# 12 Ways of Christmas

CULTIVATE A RESTFUL
(NOT STRESSFUL) SEASON

Cassia Elder

Copyright © 2021 by Cassia Elder

All rights reserved. No part of this work may be reproduced, stored in a retrieval system, or transmitted in any form or by any means—for example, electronic, photocopy, recording—without the prior written permission of the author. The only exception is brief quotations in printed reviews.

Printed in the United States of America
ISBN 9798693117099 (paperback)

Unless otherwise noted, all Scripture is taken from: The Holy Bible, New International Version®, NIV®. Copyright © 1973, 1978, 1984, 2011 by Biblica, Inc.® Used by permission. All rights reserved worldwide.

Scripture marked (ESV): The Holy Bible, English Standard Version. Copyright © 2001 by Crossway Bibles, a publishing ministry of Good News Publishers. Text Edition: 2016. All rights reserved.

Scripture marked (MSG): *The Message*. Copyright © 1993, 1994, 1995, 1996, 2000, 2001, 2002. Used by permission of NavPress Publishing Group.

Scripture marked (NLT): The Holy Bible, New Living Translation. Copyright © 1996, 2004, 2015 by Tyndale House Foundation. Used by permission of Tyndale House Publishers, Inc., Carol Stream, Illinois 60188. All rights reserved.

Scripture marked (VOICE): The Voice Bible. Copyright © 2012. Used by permission of Thomas Nelson, Inc., The Voice TM translation © 2012 Ecclesia Bible Society. All rights reserved.

Scripture marked (NASB): New American Standard Bible®. Copyright © 1960,1962,1963,1968,1971,1972,1973,1975,1977,1995 by The Lockman Foundation. Used by permission.

Scripture marked (NKJV): New King James Version®. Copyright © 1982 by Thomas Nelson. Used by permission. All rights reserved.

# Contents

Christmas JOY: Jesus, Others, You ...................5

Way 1- Jesus: Make Room .............................15

Way 2- Others: Be Present ...........................29

Way 3- You: Prepare Your Heart ...................41

Way 4- Jesus: Seek Him ..............................55

Way 5- Others: Spread the Word ..................67

Way 6- You: Choose Joy.............................79

Way 7- Jesus: Worship Him........................91

Way 8- Others: Give Intentionally................103

Way 9- You: Pursue Peace ........................115

Way 10- Jesus: Surrender to Him ..............125

Way 11- Others: Serve Selflessly ...............137

Way 12- You: Find Rest ...........................149

12 Ways for Every Day............................159

*About the Author* ...............................163

*Also from Cassia* ...............................164

# Dedication

To Grandma Phyllis,
who filled every Christmas with wonder.

# Acknowledgments

*Jesus*, I love You most. Thank You for rescuing me. You are my Redeemer.

*Chris*, thank you for loving me well, for encouraging and supporting me as I pursue my calling. I am grateful for how hard you work to give our family a good life. I love you, husband.

*Asa*, I am so proud of you. God has given you many gifts and has a good plan to use them. You are brave and strong and loyal. You make me laugh like no one else.

*Lindsey*, my dear, sweet friend and editor, you made this book so much better! You make me better. I'm grateful God brought us together.

---

NOTE: I make every effort to connect with you as transparently as possible. Our lives are purposefully and inseparably intertwined with the lives of others. So, I am also intentional to protect the hearts and the privacy of those people whose stories intersect with mine. The personal stories in this book are completely true. In most instances, friends and family have graciously granted me permission to share with you their stories and their part in my story. In some other places, I have changed names and superfluous details like locations or events for the privacy of others while maintaining the integrity of the situation.

# Christmas JOY:

# Jesus, Others, You

Christmas magic! Long before the Halloween candy gets marked down to 50%, Christmas trimmings start to line the shelves of our local superstore. I get a little twinkle in my eye and begin to dream up a picture-perfect holiday. In my vision, my family wears coordinating plaid pajamas while holding matching snowman mugs filled with gourmet hot cocoa as we sing Christmas carols in front of a brightly lit 12-foot Douglas fir worthy of the cover of Better Homes and Gardens.

Every year of my adult life the holiday season followed the same messed-up pattern. Unrealistic anticipation drove unrelenting preparation and resulted in unmet expectations. Early December visions of sugar plums left me with a post-Christmas pile of shriveled prunes. As I allowed the end of the year funk to set in, my husband punctuated, "We are not doing Christmas next year. We are just staying home alone." Some years I agreed.

Unfortunately, when the season rolled around the following year, I experienced selective amnesia about the stress of the previous holiday. With each failure, I was more certain I just needed to try harder, start earlier, plan better, spend more. Surely, "The Most Wonderful Time of the Year" was just out of reach. Grander dreams led to graver disappointments.

# 12 Ways of Christmas

I continued that pattern for more than 15 years until, one year, instead of higher hopes that brought lower letdowns, I simply stayed down. November came and went. Two weeks into December I hadn't purchased a single gift or put up a solitary decoration. I pulled every last trick out of my bag in an attempt to evoke the Christmas spirit. I shopped 'til I dropped, but I wasn't in the mood to buy a thing. I whipped out the glue dots, scrapbook paper, and glitter for a Christmas craft extravaganza at my dining room table, but it brought no cheer. I baked (and full disclosure—ate) a couple dozen of my favorite seasonal treats. My belly was full, but my heart was still empty. None of the typical activities changed my mood, because what I actually needed was a change of heart.

Over the next few years, I began to make small, incremental changes. Until one Christmas, on the drive home from our celebration travels, my husband, son, and I all agreed—that was the best Christmas we ever had. Over the following weeks and months, I began to process what was different that year, the one I will refer to as "Our First Best Christmas." If I could pin it down perhaps, I would avoid a return to the same messed-up pattern I had followed for so many years. And maybe there could be many more "Best Christmases" ahead.

My hope is that by sharing my repeated failures, as well as my key take-aways, our time together will help you to also cultivate a Christmas season that is restful, not stressful.

**Renewed Mind**

Romans 12:2 says, "Do not conform to the pattern of this world, but be transformed by the renewing of your mind. Then you will be able to test and approve what God's will is—his good, pleasing and perfect will."

# Christmas JOY: Jesus, Others, You

That messed-up pattern I had followed all those years was conforming to the pattern of the world. The New Living Translation (NLT) puts Romans 12:2 this way, "Don't copy the behavior and customs of this world, but let God transform you into a new person by changing the way you think." I tried to plan, prepare, and purchase my way to the perfect Christmas. Celebrating our Savior's birth should not leave us financially strained and emotionally drained. While searching for the Christmas spirit, I failed to live in the fullness of the Holy Spirit.

Increased effort will never be enough to effect real change. If we want to break old habits and find a different way of living, we must allow ourselves to be transformed by establishing a new, godly method of thinking. Although the world's pattern for the holiday season is hustle and bustle, God's message is peace on earth and joy to the world.

Renewing our minds begins by getting our priorities in order. Jesus spells it all out for us in Mark chapter 12. This passage, where we find what we commonly call the Greatest Commandment, will guide us throughout our time together.

"One of the teachers of the law came and heard them debating. Noticing that Jesus had given a good answer, he asked him, "Of all the commandments, which one is the most important?" "The most important one," answered Jesus, "is this 'Hear, O Israel: The Lord our God, the Lord is one. Love the Lord your God with all your heart and with all your soul and with all your mind and with all your strength.' The second is this: 'Love your neighbor as yourself.' There is no command greater than these."" Mark 12:28-31

Using these verses as a guide, we see the appropriate order in all we do is to keep Jesus first, put others' needs above our own, and care for ourselves in a balanced way.

# 12 Ways of Christmas

The path to peace and joy at Christmas is:
JOY= Jesus, Others, You

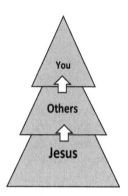

**Jesus**

"Love the Lord your God with all your heart and with all your soul and with all your mind and with all your strength." (v.30)

God wants us to love Him with every part of our lives, on Christmas day and every day. We demonstrate that love by keeping Jesus at the heart of all we do. Unless we put Him in His rightful place, we will never find peace.

The very most important thing that was different for my family the year of "Our First Best Christmas" was this: it was the most Christ-centered season I had ever celebrated. In the proceeding chapters, we will describe in practical terms how we can make Jesus the focus for the entire holiday season leading up to our traditional celebrations. We will learn to: *Make Room, Seek Him, Worship Him,* and *Surrender to Him.*

# Christmas JOY: Jesus, Others, You

### Others

Romans 12:10 says, "Be devoted to one another in love. Honor one another above yourselves." In this verse, Paul reminds us that genuine love puts others first. While I had convinced myself that everything I did every Christmas was for everyone else, my heart was self-focused. I was consumed with my own wants and needs and expectations. In all of my doing, I ended up leaving out actual connection. When the celebration was over, I was left with a messy house and an empty heart.

"Our First Best Christmas" was the most others-focused celebration to date. Together we are going to take a look at how we can love others well at Christmastime in four ways: *Be Present, Spread the Word, Give Intentionally,* and *Serve Selflessly.*

### You

Our key passage in Mark is often summed up, "Love God. Love others." This is so good, so appropriate. I use it often myself and have heard many people, who are wiser and more Biblically knowledgeable than I, say it that way as well. Now, it may sound scandalous, but I don't think it would be wrong to say it this way:

"Love God. Love others. Love yourself."

So here's Jesus answering "What is the greatest commandment?" And He says that besides loving God with all of your being, it is to "Love your neighbor *as* yourself." (Emphasis mine.) He did not say, "Love your neighbor, *not* yourself." I think Jesus made it clear that to love ourselves is an expectation, even part of the Greatest Commandment. God loves us, and He wants us to love ourselves too, in a balanced way.

# 12 Ways of Christmas

The world takes self-love and self-care to the extreme of self-obsession. The result of unbridled self-indulgence is narcissism. But the tendency we have as Christians is to run far from pride, and that can lead us to self-neglect and even self-hatred. Refusing to care for ourselves is not the equivalent of selflessness. The cure for self-focus is not ignoring our own needs. As believers, we are the temple of the Holy Spirit, and He is not interested in living in a rundown dump.

While God does not want us to be self-focused, it is also not His will for us to ignore our personal needs.

During "Our First Best Christmas," I learned there is a balance between self-obsession and self-hatred, one that can only be found as we walk in step with the Spirit. We are going to link arms and explore what it looks like to love ourselves in a balanced way throughout the Christmas festivities by doing this: *Prepare Your Heart, Choose Joy, Pursue Peace,* and *Find Rest.*

With these priorities in mind—Jesus, Others, You—we are going to dig into 12 practical ways to support a more peaceful Christmas. The *12 Ways* are not theoretical, they are action items we can implement. The concepts are simple. It's not complicated. But this is not the easy way out; it will be hard work.

Let's renew our minds to pursue peace and joy this holiday season, as we set our priorities right for a transformed Christmas experience.

BEFORE WE GET STARTED:
I almost subtitled this book "*A Practical Guide to* a Restful (Not Stressful) Season." But I opted for the word *Cultivate.* In this book, you will find tools and suggestions for practical application in each of the *12 Ways.* I will share specific strategies that worked for my family. However, this is not a quick-fix, step-by-step manual to instantaneously overhaul your holiday. Trying to drastically change everything all at

once can actually cause more stress and frustration than leaving things as they've always been. The *12 Ways* are not a one-time Christmas makeover. The change that resulted in "Our First Best Christmas" didn't happen overnight or even in a single season. Creating a sustainable difference requires small, incremental changes.

After finally experiencing a restful holiday, I was tempted to try to recreate the previous season using my observations of what worked as a cookie-cutter. The *12 Ways of Christmas* are not a checklist. Instead, they are principles and postures that will cultivate change, causing it to develop and grow over time.

A word of caution: I am not in control of every element of my family's holiday celebrations and neither are you for yours. That's because our celebrations usually involve other people. Families with different traditions and schedules and preferences coming together can either be a source of conflict or an opportunity to compromise. When it comes to implementing the principles, we each need to consider our personal family dynamics. You may have to engage in a discussion about changes you would like to make. You may simply have to change what you can, and compromise where possible. Accept what you cannot change, and set boundaries around what is non-negotiable. As we continue, I hope you will find that the most important changes will take place in your own heart.

NAVIGATING THE BOOK:

Included in each of the *12 Ways* will be a Bible narrative, a personal story, and the practical application of the principle. After unpacking what each *Way* looks like lived out, I will share specific examples that worked for my family and others. These are not a task list, but ideas that may or may not work for your specific situation. There are three ways you can apply the illustrations shared in the chapters to come.

# 12 Ways of Christmas

**\*Adopt.** Take the example in the book, and use it as is.
**\*Adapt.** Change up the example, and make it your own.
**\*Adlib.** Start from scratch, and come up with an original.

At the end of each chapter, you will find 3 sections to help you apply what you've learned.

**\*Pray.** A simple prayer asking God to help you put the ideas into practice.
**\*Meditate or Memorize.** Verses on the topic to help you remember the truth.
**\*Consider.** Five questions for personal reflection that can also be used for group discussion.

I am so glad you are joining me on this journey to cultivate a restful, Christ-centered Christmas season!

**PRAY:**
*Lord, teach me to cultivate a season that is restful, not stressful, by loving You, loving others, and loving myself. Help me to put You first, to consider others' needs above my own, and to care for myself in a way that is honoring to You. In Jesus' name, amen.*

**MEDITATE OR MEMORIZE:**
"Do not conform to the pattern of this world, but be transformed by the renewing of your mind. Then you will be able to test and approve what God's will is—his good, pleasing and perfect will." Romans 12:2

"The most important one," answered Jesus, "is this 'Hear, O Israel: The Lord our God, the Lord is one. Love the Lord your God with all your heart and with all your soul and with all

## Christmas JOY: Jesus, Others, You

your mind and with all your strength.' The second is this: 'Love your neighbor as yourself.' There is no command greater than these.'" Mark 12:29-31

"But the angel said to them, 'Do not be afraid. I bring you good news that will cause great joy for all people. Today in the town of David a Savior has been born to you; he is the Messiah, the Lord. This will be a sign to you: You will find a baby wrapped in cloths and lying in a manger." Suddenly a great company of the heavenly host appeared with the angel, praising God and says, 'Glory to God in the highest heaven, and on earth peace to those on whom his favor rests.'" Luke 2:10-14

**CONSIDER:**
1. How does a dreamed-up, picture-perfect Christmas compare to your reality?

2. Think back over previous holiday seasons. How have you experienced- unrealistic anticipation, unrelenting preparation, unmet expectations?

3. In what ways have your Christmas celebrations been following the patterns of this world?

4. Which do you find most difficult- putting Jesus first, putting others' needs above your own, or caring for yourself in a balanced way?

5. What comes to mind when you consider renewing your mind to pursue peace and joy?

# Way 1- Jesus:

# Make Room

"In those days Caesar Augustus issued a decree that a census should be taken of the entire Roman world. (This was the first census that took place while Quirinius was governor of Syria.) And everyone went to their own town to register.

So Joseph also went up from the town of Nazareth in Galilee to Judea, to Bethlehem the town of David, because he belonged to the house and line of David. He went there to register with Mary, who was pledged to be married to him and was expecting a child. While they were there, the time came for the baby to be born, and she gave birth to her firstborn, a son. She wrapped him in cloths and placed him in a manger, because there was no guest room available for them."
Luke 2:1-7

I don't remember seeing any kid volunteer to play the innkeeper at the annual church Christmas pageant. Whoever gets stuck with that role has to turn away a woman who is very obviously near to giving birth. But this is not just any pregnant woman. She's the one who is preparing to bring the Messiah into the world. Even though it's just a play, you know that kid gets dirty looks. Seriously?! You couldn't make room for Jesus? I would definitely give up my own bed and go sleep with the sheep to provide a place for the Savior to be born!

# 12 Ways of Christmas

We don't know for sure if there really was an innkeeper. But just in case, we probably ought to give the guy a little slack. The Bible does not give us an indication that anyone besides Mary, Joseph, and Elizabeth knew the baby Mary was carrying would be the promised Messiah. The city was jam-packed. Everyone from the lineage of David had come to Bethlehem at the same time for the same reason as Mary and Joseph—the census ordered by Caesar Augustus. They didn't call ahead to book a room. But even if they did, we know from *Seinfeld*, it's not so much the taking of the reservation, but the keeping of the reservation.

We may look back a little judgy at the people who did not make room for the Messiah over 2000 years ago. But we have the whole of Scripture and two millennia of history to inform us of who Jesus is, and still, we are guilty of not making room for Him.

## Birthday Party

One sunny May afternoon, my family attended the 90th birthday celebration of our dear friend, Lannie. The party was an open-house held in the reception hall of the little white church just up the road. When we arrived, the line of people waiting to greet the guest of honor extended out the door, down the sidewalk, and into the church parking lot. Lannie, perched in his old rocking chair, was the center of the celebration. Every person in attendance was there to see him, to honor him, to celebrate him. You know the day was all about Lannie when the entire room sang the traditional song and inserted his name after "Happy birthday, dear..." Another line formed to say goodbye as the party was winding down. Of course, in between, he was showered with gifts and served plenty of food and drinks.

# Way 1-Jesus: Make Room

Wouldn't it be weird if we pushed up to the door of the church hall, squeezed past the reception line, and headed straight for the cake?

What if we left the party without talking to Lannie?

Strangest of all, what if we decided to celebrate his birthday on our own? Like, if we put a picture of him on the mantle, planned a party, and called it "Lannie Day." But we didn't bother to invite him and never mentioned him.

Yes. I'm pretty sure you would agree that would be weird, and you can probably see where I'm going with this.

I did it for years. And I know I'm not alone. Every December, parties are hosted supposedly in honor of Jesus' birthday, but he never gets an invitation. We celebrate Jesus on a holiday that bears His name by topping our tree with an angel or displaying a historically inaccurate manger scene on the end table, and that's the extent of His involvement. Maybe we attend church like we do every other Sunday or simply to fulfill our twice-a-year obligation. But how are we including Him in the celebration? How are we inviting Him in?

The world's pattern for Christmas revolves around food and family and gifts. All of these things are good. But a renewed mind makes Jesus the center. For all those years of Christmas fails, leaving Christ out of my Christmas celebration is the #1 reason it was stressful.

Let's invite Jesus to the party! He's the one we're celebrating!

Have you ever had an unexpected guest arrive for Christmas dinner after the table was already set? Maybe, cousin Emily showed up with her new boyfriend unannounced. The whole family scrambled to squeeze him in. Uncle Jim retrieved Grandma's squeaky rocking chair from down the hall, the one that was only used for decoration, and no one ever dares to sit in it. There was not an extra setting of

## 12 Ways of Christmas

the good china that only comes out on Christmas, so Aunt Lynn grabbed the green plastic plate her family used for every day. Everyone skootched their seats a few inches so the plate and chair would fit at the table. It was elbow to elbow, a little uncomfortable, and totally awkward.

Jesus should not be an afterthought; He's the guest of honor. His presence at our celebration shouldn't be unexpected, and we sure don't want to make Him feel uninvited. We can't set the table with all of our plans and ideas and traditions, then squeeze Him in at the last minute. We need to make room for Jesus by putting Him first. Let's invite Him in, make Him feel welcome, and honor Him at the heart of everything we do.

My birthday celebrations as a child included a special birthday dinner and a few gifts from my parents and grandparents. And cake. Always cake! Most years for my son's birthday, I have tried to make an event of the entire day. He wakes up to balloons and streamers or the sound of an air horn or cake for breakfast. Yes, always cake!
But one year my child insisted it was his birthday week. He wanted to go out to eat several times, binge-watch all his favorites, stay up to the wee hours, sleep through mid-day, and skip the school work. Every day for the entire week. I guess that's not so unusual these days. I have a few friends who enjoy a month-long birthday fest.

The Bible does not give us the exact date of Jesus' birth. December is not likely the time when Jesus was actually born, but it is the season when we traditionally celebrate His birth. So why not make Him the heart of it? If anyone deserves to be celebrated during their entire birthday month, it's Jesus!

# Way 1- Jesus: Make Room

**What does it look like to Make Room for Jesus?**

To *Make Room for Jesus* means not just squeezing Him in, but loving Him with all our being by putting Him first. First in our hearts, in our celebrations, and throughout the holiday season. We know that we make time for what truly matters to us. "I don't have time," is simply an excuse that really communicates, "It's not important to me." Let's be honest, we'll spend 15 minutes waiting in line for an overpriced latte, half an hour scrolling through Facebook, and never miss an episode of *The Voice*, but how much time do we give our relationship with God? Making Room for Jesus is more important than carving out an hour for a workout or coffee with a friend.

I was always that kid who looked forward to school, especially test-taking. Weird, right? What you may find equally weird is that back when I worked in the factory, I actually enjoyed attending mandatory safety training. I eagerly listened during one such training session, when the instructor began by sharing his daily routine. Each morning before coming to work, he made it a priority to eat breakfast. After all, it is the most important meal of the day. But on occasion, he would oversleep. Breakfast would be skipped, and he would bear the consequence of a grumbling stomach until lunchtime.

He continued to say, however, that no matter how late he was for work in the morning, he never once ran out the door thinking, "I just don't have time to put on pants today." You see, breakfast is a priority, but wearing pants—that is a value. The safety leader went on to relate his amusing analogy to how safety in the workplace should be more than just a priority; it has to be a value. A priority is something that, while important, can be set aside if it becomes inconvenient or there's simply not time. A value is foundational, and cannot be discarded at any cost.

# 12 Ways of Christmas

I told you, it never worked out for me when I tried to plan, prepare, and purchase my way to the perfect Christmas. That is because Jesus is the reason for the season (cue the *DC Talk* tune) and the reason for our being. All the other things we try to fill our lives with leave us emptier and wanting more. Trying to do life without Him will no doubt result in a season of stress. Cultivating a Christmas that is restful means making room for Jesus must be not just a priority, but a value. True rest only comes in relationship and communion with Him.

MAKE ROOM IN YOUR HEART:
   *Relationship**. Every person reading this book, every human who has ever existed, every one of us is made in the image of God, and He loves us. But our sin separates us from relationship with Him. Sin may sound like one of those churchy words you've heard tossed around without much explanation. Simply put, it is falling short of God's perfect standard, and if we are honest with ourselves, each of us would admit we have done that.

God demonstrated His love for us by sending His Only Son Jesus to restore our relationship with Himself. Through Jesus' sacrificial death on the cross, God offers the forgiveness of our sins and the gift of eternal life with Him in Heaven.

Maybe you picked up this Christmas book and you're not quite sure about all this Jesus stuff. That's okay. If that is you, I'm so glad you have continued with me this far. I have been praying specifically for you. I want to tell you a little bit about the free gift from God available to us through Jesus. The gift of forgiveness of our sins, of restored relationship with God, and of eternal life with Him.

The entire Bible is the story of God's love and pursuit of restored relationship with humanity. We could not possibly read and unpack that whole thing right now. But I want to share kind of a brief explanation of what it looks like to have a relationship with God through receiving Jesus.

# Way 1- Jesus: Make Room

Romans 10:9 says "If you declare with your mouth, 'Jesus is Lord,' and believe in your heart that God raised him from the dead, you will be saved."

Now, I hope not to oversimplify this, but I also don't want to overwhelm you with information. So today we are just going to plant some seeds with kind of a basic summary of the path to salvation. And I'm going to make it easy to remember with ABC.

> A. **Admit** you are a sinner and repent, or turn away, from your sin understanding there is a price to pay. Know that you cannot be good enough or pay the debt on your own.
> B. **Believe** God sent His only Son, Jesus, to die in your place to pay the price for your sin. Jesus rose again from the grave so you could be in relationship with the Father.
> C. **Commit** to making Jesus the Lord, or Authority, over your life, accepting the free gift of salvation.

You are going to read a lot more in this book about God and what it looks like to live in relationship with Him through Jesus. Whether you are ready to make that decision now, or you need more time to process what all of this means for you, I want to share a prayer you can pray.

*Dear God, thank You for creating me for the purpose of relationship with You. I understand my sin separates me from that relationship. I admit my sin, and I choose today to turn from it. I believe You sent Your only Son Jesus to pay the penalty for my sin. I want to accept the gift of forgiveness and salvation. I commit my life to You; please teach me to follow You. In Jesus' name, amen.*

If you have never done it before, I want to invite you to make room for Jesus in your heart and in your life. Make Him the center. Accept the greatest gift—the one He left Heaven and came to earth to give—the free gift of Salvation.

# 12 Ways of Christmas

**\*Communion.** Although a wedding usually ends shortly after the vows, the ceremony is just the beginning of a marriage. Praying a salvation prayer, accepting Jesus as our Savior, and committing our lives to Him, is just the beginning of the relationship. Life with Jesus continues with ongoing connection and continued growth. Growing up, I always heard the term "Jesus is my Lord and Savior." The Savior part is easy to accept. However, salvation is not just about what God saved us from but more so what He saved us for. Jesus came to be Immanuel, God with us, and to give us abundant life in relationship with Him. That's where making Jesus our Lord comes in, and that's a little harder for us to process. It's not difficult to get on board with letting Jesus rescue us from an eternity separated from Him in a literal Hell. But making Him our Lord means submitting to His will and allowing Him full authority over our lives to direct our steps, to govern our actions. Making room for Jesus in our hearts means genuine fellowship, putting Him first, and allowing Him to lead us.

MAKE ROOM IN YOUR CELEBRATIONS:

A few ways my family has focused our celebrations on Jesus over the years is by reading Luke 2 aloud before opening gifts, singing our favorite Christmas hymn, or attending church together. Depending on your personal group dynamic and your freedom to shape celebrations, this may look different. Maybe those you gather with won't agree to any of these ideas. Know that whether or not you are able to include Jesus in your collective activities, you are always able to honor God in your heart and include Him in your individual celebration.

I wanted to find a way to include Jesus in the festivities at our home when we get together with our kids and grandkids. So, several years ago, we started a new holiday tradition. Christmas is celebrating Jesus' birth, after all, and a birthday party calls for birthday cake. Yes. Because as you heard me say before. Always cake! Jesus' birthday cake has become a

# Way 1-Jesus: Make Room

favorite part of the celebration for our family. We've had a cookie cake with a frosting greeting, "Happy Birthday Jesus," or green and red sprinkled cupcakes, or a traditional cake topped with a dollar store Nativity set. We gather around, sometimes light a candle, and always sing at the top of our lungs. "Happy birthday to You. Happy birthday to You. Happy birthday, dear Jesus. Happy birthday to You!"

MAKE ROOM THROUGHOUT THE SEASON:
 **\*Devotional Time.** Relationships require time and attention. Growing in our walk with Jesus is a commitment to connecting with Him every day. If you do not already have an established devotional routine, you might be a little bit skeptical about setting aside dedicated time every day to spend with Jesus this Christmas. I mean, isn't this book supposed to be about making life during the holidays less stressful? And now rather than lightening the load, I'm asking you to add one more thing. Maybe you're thinking that giving your time and attention to Jesus sounds great, but how 'bout we make that a New Year's resolution? Because ain't nobody got time for that during the holidays. It's okay if you're feeling that way.

 Even well-established routines and habits can get derailed during the holidays. We let our sleep schedules, our eating plans, our spiritual disciplines slide. I had a regular rhythm of prayer and Bible study. But for several Christmases, when my calendar was already packed, I added in all the holiday activities, and I crowded Jesus out. Some days I would wake up in a rush, anxious to check off every last box on my to-do list. "Good morning, Jesus. I'll catch You later when everything else is done." Where did the day go? Little got accomplished, but still, I was spent. "Good night, Jesus. I promise, tomorrow I'll spend time with You." But God wants the best of us, not what's left of us.

# 12 Ways of Christmas

Perhaps you know the story, the one about Jesus feeding the 5,000. Jesus and His disciples were headed across the sea in a boat. The people from the village could see where the boat was headed, so they ran ahead to meet Jesus there. They hadn't stopped to pack a lunch; they just went after Jesus. We read in Matthew 14, as evening approached, Jesus' companions told Him to send the people away to get food, but Jesus said, "They do not need to go away. You give them something to eat."

Andrew, one of the disciples, spoke up. "Here is a boy with five small barley loaves and two fish, but how far will they go among so many?" John 6:9

How far will they go among so many? Those words resonate with me. Look, there are only 24 hours in a day, and I absolutely must sleep for a bare minimum of 8 of them in order to function at all. That leaves 16 hours at best. But how far will they go among so many? So many projects. So many commitments. So many obligations. So many dreams. Add in all the Christmas to-do's, and I have spread myself thin. I spend my days trudging through life like I'm knee-deep in wet concrete. How far can the little bit I have go among so many?

What about the young boy who gave His lunch to Jesus? Exactly how far did it go? Well, Jesus took the modest meal that was given to Him, and He multiplied it. Those five meager loaves of bread and two measly fish went on to feed 5,000 men, plus women and children.

The people ran to meet with Jesus, and He provided.

"When they had all had enough to eat, he said to his disciples, 'Gather the pieces that are left over. Let nothing be wasted.' So they gathered them and filled twelve baskets with the pieces of the five barley loaves left over by those who had eaten." John 6:12-13

That's right. After the entire crowd was satisfied by the miraculous meal, there was, in fact, a surplus. More left over

# Way 1- Jesus: Make Room

than there had been to start. Because what we give to Jesus, He multiplies.

Our lives are typically over-scheduled and under-rested before we pile on baking and shopping and decorating and viewing lights and attending performances and whatever else your Christmas festivities entail. It sounds counter-intuitive to set aside more time for Jesus when we list all the things that already don't fit into the few short hours. But we can trust Him with our time and our energy. When we run to meet with Him, He will provide. Because what we give to Jesus, He multiplies.

Making room for Jesus doesn't dictate that we don't decorate or bake or shop. It means we make Him the center and more than a priority, a value. We manage our schedules around our time with Him. If that time needs to be a line item on the itinerary to make sure it happens, then we write it down first and fill in the calendar around it.

When we seek Him first, give Him the best of our time and our energy, at the end of the day we are not depleted. We are miraculously satisfied, and in fact, have a surplus. You see, what we give to Jesus, He multiplies. And honestly, we will have more left over than we had to start.

In *Way 4: Seek Him* we will talk more in-depth about some specific, practical ways to implement spiritual disciplines and devotional practices. Until then, determine to make room for Jesus by setting aside time in your day.

**\*Remove.** Making room for Jesus may including removing the things that are crowding Him out. Take an inventory. What is making your schedule so overfilled that there is no room left for Jesus? What could you remove or set aside during the holiday season to create margin? For me, it looks like being careful with my "Yes" and reducing time-wasters like binging Netflix and scrolling through Facebook.

# 12 Ways of Christmas

Let's open the doors of our hearts and our lives this Christmas to not only make room for Jesus but to give Him the place of honor. Put Him first. Include Him in everything. In the chapters that follow, we will look at 3 more ways to make Jesus the center of all we do as we celebrate His birthday.

**PRAY:**
*Jesus, thank You for coming from Heaven to earth to be Immanuel, God with us. Help me not to take that for granted. Teach me to make room for You this holiday season. Remind me that You are the reason we celebrate and the reason we live. Jesus, I invite You in. To my celebrations, to my preparation, to every aspect of my life. May I put You first and honor You in all I do this Christmas. It is in Your name I pray, amen.*

**MEDITATE OR MEMORIZE:**
"She wrapped him in cloths and placed him in a manger, because there was no guest room available for them." Luke 2:7b

"If you declare with your mouth, 'Jesus is Lord,' and believe in your heart that God raised him from the dead, you will be saved." Romans 10:9

"'The virgin will conceive and give birth to a son, and they will call him Immanuel' (which means 'God with us')." Matthew 1:23

**CONSIDER:**
1. What does it mean for you personally to make room for Jesus in your heart?

# Way 1- Jesus: Make Room

2. List some ways you can make room for Jesus in your celebrations this Christmas.

3. Describe your devotional time on a typical day. Is it different during the holidays?

4. How would it look for you to make time with Jesus a value and not just a priority?

5. What might be crowding Jesus out of your day that may have to be removed for a season?

# Way 2- Others:

# Be Present

"As Jesus and his disciples were on their way, he came to a village where a woman named Martha opened her home to him. She had a sister called Mary, who sat at the Lord's feet listening to what he said. But Martha was distracted by all the preparations that had to be made. She came to him and asked, 'Lord, don't you care that my sister has left me to do the work by myself? Tell her to help me!' 'Martha, Martha,' the Lord answered, 'you are worried and upset about many things, but few things are needed—or indeed only one. Mary has chosen what is better, and it will not be taken away from her.'" Luke 10:38-42

What in the world does that passage have to do with Christmas? Aren't all the Christmas verses isolated to the first two chapters of Matthew and Luke? Did you wonder if a page from another book got slipped in here by accident?

If only that were the case. The story of Mary and Martha may not sound very Christmasy to most, but it is an unfortunately accurate description of how many of my Christmas celebrations have played out.

Martha made room for Jesus. She opened her home to Him and invited Him in. Then she was too busy to spend time with Him. In chapters ahead, we will see how this relates to our

# 12 Ways of Christmas

own relationship with Jesus and the importance of what we do in our time with Him. But the focus of this chapter *Way 2* is how to love others well and put their needs above our own by being present with them at Christmas.

Being present with others, giving them our full attention, shows them they are seen and heard and valued and loved. They are important enough that we can set aside everything else to give them our time. Food is my love language and giving gifts gets me giddy, but connecting with my people is a vital part of a stress-free season.

**Choose Better**

Year after year the same scenario went down at my home on Christmas. As my husband and son sat in the living room laughing and playing with our grandkids, my huffing and slamming around in the kitchen got louder. And there were times that, like Martha, I tattletaled to God about it. "I'm doing all this work by myself and nobody appreciates me. If he had even lifted a finger, everything would have been done before they got here. Why don't you make him help?" Oh, I can hear Jesus now, "Cassia, Cassia, you are worried and upset about many things. He has chosen what is better."

Martha chose. Mary chose. It was a conscious choice for one sister to be more concerned about the food and for the other to be more concerned about fellowship.

My idea of the perfect Christmas was rooted in my childhood. Every year, on December 24$^{th,}$ we dressed in our Sunday best and packed into the family car headed for Grandma Phyllis' and Grandpa Red's house. For that one night of every year, their little ranch home was transformed into a Holiday Wonderland. Multicolored, egg-sized lights that edged their roofline could be seen from a mile away. A record of all our yuletide favorites sung by Bing Crosby

# Way 2- Others: Be Present

rotated on the turntable. The artificial spruce grew a little thicker, as Grandma had sprayed it with a fresh coat of flocking. A fancy punch bowl was filled with eggnog that we sipped from matching crystal cups. Every horizontal surface in the kitchen was covered with an over-the-top feast that extended into the dining room where Grandma placed all my favorites. Buckeyes and toffee and fudge. Oh my!

I dreamed of a Christmas filled with such wonder for our kids and grandkids. I thought magic of that sort could only be achieved if I recreated the Christmas scene from my memories. I strived to live up to Grandma's example—to do all the things, and be all the things.

Every detail was painstakingly laid out in my Christmas planner. Besides my gift list, I documented what I would wear to each of our celebrations. My plans included a chart of the food items I would prepare, the dish they'd be presented in, and where they would be placed on the table. Y'all, somebody has to set the schedules and make the food. But I allowed obsession over preparation to distract me from living in the moment.

When our family gathered to celebrate, I wasn't just worried about the decorations and food. I missed most of the gift opening because I was busy grabbing every scrap of wrapping paper as soon as it was ripped from the package. When the pile of presents under the tree was depleted, I hurried back to the kitchen to pack up leftovers and start on the mountain of dishes.

It is not others-focused to be so busy doing for people that we fail to be with people. And while I convinced myself that this was my way of serving my family, the truth is, it had become more about me. The drive for holiday perfection came from my self-focused need to be in control.

I told you previously that my greatest mistake at Christmas was not putting Jesus first. My second biggest failure was not truly connecting with others. Like Martha, I was so distracted by all the preparations, I rushed through the season without pausing to be present. While evaluating what was different "Our First Best Christmas," I realized the impact of others-focus. I chose to prioritize being over doing. I chose to be present. I chose what was better.

To be consumed by distraction is the world's pattern for Christmas. But being present in the moment is a sign of a renewed mind. When we choose fellowship like Mary, the connection will not be taken away from us.

If you haven't figured it out already, my Grandma Phyllis was a bit of a Martha. She didn't complain and throw a fit like I did. But she did miss out by being in the kitchen with the food instead of in the living room with her loved ones.

After Grandpa passed, and as our family continued to grow, Christmas started to look a little different. Between juggling our own traditions at home with Asa, gathering with our grandkids, and all the other family get-togethers, we had no less than six (but sometimes more) separate Christmas celebrations. To manage all the activity, we had to adjust our holiday schedule, and we no longer went to Grandma's house on the night before Christmas with our extended family. Instead, Chris, Asa, and I visited Grandma by ourselves late in the morning on Christmas Eve.

I will always cherish those childhood memories of a full house and a big buffet and presents piled high. But I also recall fondly the new memories made on the Christmases alone with Grandma, just her and my immediate family. We brought a simple breakfast bread to share and opened a handful of presents, one at a time. The conversation was rich as we had Grandma's undivided attention, and she had ours. Simplifying and embracing a slower rhythm for Christmas allowed us to be present in a way we never had before.

Let's not be too critical of Martha and Grandma. And we shouldn't be so hard on ourselves if we're the Martha in our family. We need to understand that this behavior comes from

# Way 2- Others: Be Present

a servant's heart—the desire to show love to our people through acts of service. But when service becomes our identity and we allow it to take precedence over the people we are serving, it is no longer others-focused. Valuing productivity over presence prevents us from loving others well.

### What does it look like to Be Present with Others?

To *Be Present with Others* means to be engaged by giving our full attention to the people who are with us in the moment. Being present is a choice. It is one practical way we can actively live out "love your neighbor."

The food will be consumed, the gift wrap will be tossed, and the dishes will always be there. But the opportunity to make memories and be present with our people is fleeting. When all the décor is stuffed away, what is left will be determined by the choices we made. We can have memories for ourselves and an impact on the lives of others or we can be consumed by distraction.

BE PRESENT IN YOUR CELEBRATIONS:
  \*Simplify. Jesus told Martha, "You are worried and upset about many things, but few things are needed, or indeed only one." Martha made it too complicated and was worried about things that don't matter. What really matters to you and your family?
  Perhaps a feast like Grandma Phyllis's is an important part of your Christmas tradition. For our family, I was the only one who was intent on having an elaborate meal. The kids were too excited about opening presents and playing together to sit still and eat much. I ended up with a fridge full of leftovers and a good portion of the food got thrown away. So we made a few changes over the years to simplify our celebrations. One year we had a pizza picnic on the living room floor.

# 12 Ways of Christmas

Sometimes we did a pitch-in or quick-prep foods. Instead of toiling in the kitchen, I could be present with my family as soon as they arrived. And my grandma might have been disappointed to see that we used paper plates instead of the good china. But it allowed me to be more concerned about my guests than the mess. Rather than lamenting over a mountain of dirty dishes, I was present at the table playing games or helping one of the children unbox a 12" doll held tight by 20 zip-ties.

For a couple of years, another way our family chose to simplify was by spending the money set aside for Christmas presents on a trip with our grandkids. Each child still got a couple of small gifts and their stocking stuffed with goodies, but the main present was an overnight stay at an indoor water park. This made the season much less stressful for me, cutting my shopping by more than half. Because there were fewer presents to unwrap, we had more time together after dinner, and we continued to enjoy each other during our trip. Prioritizing memories over material is elemental to a restful Christmas.

**\*Limit distractions.** "But Martha was distracted by _____." Fill in the blank. What distracts you from being present? It may be different for each of us. Besides all the preparations, I have plenty of other distractions.

I needed to hear this, and maybe you do too. Turn off the TV. Put the devices down. There. I said it.

Watching a sporting event or a movie together can be a fun way to spend family time. But if you've got the TV muted so you can keep one eye on the game and the other on the gift opening, you are not being present. But that's easy for me to say; the television isn't the screen that woos me.

A smartphone has too many benefits to mention. But ,friend, since I got my first one less than a decade ago, that thing has been going to battle for my attention. It has been my #1 distraction in recent years, and I am certain I'm not alone.

# Way 2- Others: Be Present

This practical tool designed to simplify our lives has also served to complicate them. On many Christmases, I spent more time looking through the lens of my camera than being engaged with my people. And taking pictures hasn't been the bulk of the problem. Constantly checking social media to keep a tally of who liked and commented on those pictures is honestly what kept me from being present.

Even with my fingers crossed behind my back, I can't tell you I have conquered this beast. But I have implemented a few strategies over the years to help me mitigate the distraction of my cellphone, and they might help you, too. Instead of snapping duplicate shots with my own phone, I ask our girls to share their pictures. I started wearing a watch again. (It's more than just a cute piece of jewelry.) It keeps me from picking up my phone every fifteen minutes to "see what time it is" then scrolling through Facebook for half an hour without ever having checked the time. Most drastic of all, one Christmas when we gathered, I simply turned my device OFF. Yep, that button on the side is not reserved for rebooting your phone after you let the battery die. I did it. It wasn't easy, but it was worth it. Turning my phone off helped me realize I had not been using it as a tool; it had become an idol.

Look, these are some tips that helped me reduce the amount of time I spend looking at my phone. But the truth is, the only thing that will keep our screens from consuming us is self-control. Will we allow our devices to get more of our attention than the people who we have gathered with? We must choose better and not allow distraction to get in the way of connection.

**\*Lean into relationship.** Being present is more than occupying the same space at the same time. If we truly want to connect with our people, we need to lean into relationship. Be intentionally engaged in moments that become memories.

Mary sat at the Lord's feet listening to what He had to say. I struggle with this sometimes. Not just the sitting still part,

## 12 Ways of Christmas

but also listening. When someone else is speaking, I often find myself waiting for my turn to talk; I'm busy formulating my response or framing my addition to the conversation. Active listening means paying attention to what the other person is saying.

Did you know communication is only 10% words and 90% other, non-verbal factors? Even when you're not the one doing the talking, you are saying something with your body language. Making eye contact shows you are giving attention. The other person will feel heard when your facial expressions reflect their narrative. Gestures like leaning forward and nodding demonstrate you are tuned in.

Ask good questions. I've seen plenty of dialogue die after the words, "How's work?" Leaning into relationship requires getting past the small talk and having real conversations. Asking good questions is a great way to get an exchange started, but it is also valuable in the middle of a discussion to show interest in what the other person is saying. For some people, asking good questions comes naturally. But for those of us (yes, me) who notoriously monopolize the conversation, it takes a little practice. Loving others well is a process of continually learning.

BE PRESENT THROUGHOUT THE SEASON:

We need reminders to be present during our Christmas celebrations and throughout the season as we are bombarded with activity and distraction. It's easy to overlook or take for granted the people right in front of us. How can we practice the posture of being present every day during the holidays?

**\*With your family and friends.** "Two are better than one, because they have a good return for their labor."
Ecclesiastes 4:9

We are better together! The Christmas to-do list is real, but you don't have to conquer it alone. Most activities go a little faster and are totally more fun with good company. It has

# Way 2- Others: Be Present

become a favorite tradition to go post-Thanksgiving shopping with my mom and sister-in-law. Afterward, we hang out and wrap a few of our gifts. We make memories while checking all the boxes.

Why not turn a task into a party? With a tree trimming bash at Grandma Jan's and a cookie exchange between friends, we minimized the chores and maximized the cheer!

Getting everything done during the holiday season requires a little bit of multitasking. It's easy to double up with activities that use different parts of our brains, like wrapping presents and watching a Christmas movie. But activities that use the same part of our brain, like having a conversation and checking email, really can't be done at the same time. Often, we think we're multitasking, but what actually happens is quickly switching back-and-forth between two different tasks. And when this happens, neither one gets done as well as if we had given each undertaking our full concentration.

Remember, this whole chapter is about loving others well by being present. While we can sometimes multitask with people, is also important to occasionally give our undivided attention.

**\*Wherever you are.** When Jesus said, "love your neighbor," He wasn't referring exclusively to the family next door. Every interaction is an opportunity to be a blessing. Being present every day during the season is not just a practice for our homes, but everywhere we go. As we make our way through each day, whether we are running errands or attending events, we will encounter other people there. We won't forge deep relationships with every person who crosses our paths, but we can give them our attention in the moment to show their value as human beings made in the image of God. Wherever you are, be fully there.

# 12 Ways of Christmas

During our celebrations and throughout the season, let's put others' needs above our own by giving them our attention. The best gift we can give is to be present.

**PRAY:**
*Father God, I know being present is a choice; I want to choose what is better. This Christmas, help me to simplify where I can. Reveal the distractions I need to put away. Teach me to lean into relationship, making the people in my life feel seen and heard and valued and loved throughout the season. In Jesus' name, amen.*

**MEDITATE OR MEMORIZE:**
"Martha, Martha," the Lord answered, "you are worried and upset about many things, but few things are needed—or indeed only one. Mary has chosen what is better, and it will not be taken away from her." Luke 10:41-42

"Two are better than one, because they have a good return for their labor." Ecclesiastes 4:9

"Be devoted to one another in love. Honor one another above yourselves." Romans 12:10

**CONSIDER:**
1. What would simplifying your celebrations look like for your family?

2. Name the distractions that are keeping you from being present with others. How will you limit these?

## Way 2 - Others: Be Present

3. In what ways could you be more intentional to lean into relationship?

4. Which of the activities on your Christmas agenda would be "better together"? Who might you include?

5. How could you be more present throughout the season?

# Way 3- You:

# Prepare Your Heart

"The LORD said to Moses, "Speak to the Israelites and say to them: 'These are my appointed festivals, the appointed festivals of the LORD, which you are to proclaim as sacred assemblies.'" So Moses announced to the Israelites the appointed festivals of the Lord." Leviticus 23:1-2, 44

In Leviticus 23, God delivers, through Moses, the ordained event calendar for His chosen people. These festivals, also called holy days, are where we get the word *holiday*. (Grandma Phyllis would probably appreciate that the ESV translates this word *feast*.) Besides a weekly observation of the Sabbath, seven annual occasions were to be commemorated on designated days each year. God's appointed holiday agenda, found in verses three to forty-three of this passage, consisted of thorough instructions for every aspect of the celebration. This included specifics like when to meet, what to eat, where to sleep, and which gifts to bring. These holy days were marked by order and reverence and attention to detail.

Those of us in Christ have been adopted into the family of God. And even today, He still desires that His chosen people would engage in a regular rhythm of holy days. But unlike the Israelite sacred days, He has not given us a blueprint for how

## 12 Ways of Christmas

to celebrate Christmas. From reading the accounts of those Old Testament festivals, we understand God's attitude toward our celebrations.

God prescribes celebration.
God cares about the details of celebration.
God desires to be the center of our celebration.

Times of festivity are not just good; they are commanded by God for His glory and our enjoyment. These holy days are also to be consecrated, set apart for praise and remembrance of the Lord's faithfulness. Each occasion is purposefully rooted in our relationship with God and our relationships with each other. They are opportunities to practice loving Him with all our being and loving our neighbor as ourselves.

The solution for overcoming the stress of Christmas is not to forgo the celebrations altogether, although my family seriously considered it after more than a decade of Christmas fails. The appointed festivals were described as sacred assemblies—days for getting together and gathering in community. And that is still the purpose today. The answer is to cultivate a restful season by transforming the holidays back into holy days that are honoring to God. Throughout our time together, we will look at practical external activities that will help us achieve a more Christ-centered, others-focused season. But lasting change happens from the inside out. Our hearts are the first things to prepare in pursuit of a restful Christmas.

### Preparing My Comeback

People start the countdown to Christmas earlier each year. I'm pretty sure that back in January, I saw this meme featuring Will Ferrell as *Elf* that said, "It's only 348 days 'til Christmas!" I often begin my next year's Christmas shopping as soon as the holiday goodies go on clearance. "Christmas in

# Way 3- You: Prepare Your Heart

July" kicks off the sales season each year. And the holiday interrogation begins the day after Thanksgiving, when complete strangers grill us with the imposing question, "Are you ready for Christmas?" Christmas has been on the same date every single year for my entire life. In fact, it has been a federal holiday in the United States since 1870. But for some reason, December 25th still seems to sneak up on us every year.

The ticking clock showed 15 minutes until we had to leave for our Christmas get-together. There I stood, mouth gaping, in front of the bathroom mirror. You probably know the look. As I stretched my right eye open wide to apply eyeliner, my mouth unwittingly followed suit. Meanwhile, I was rehearsing an imaginary argument in my head. Normally, I try to avoid confrontational people. But at the holidays, we don't always get to choose who we gather with. This particular Christmas, I anticipated an uncomfortable exchange. One too many times I had been caught off guard by harsh words. I can never come up with a witty response in the moment. No, the perfect comeback usually occurs to me when I'm tossing and turning, milling over the offense when I should be sound asleep. But not this time; I decided to be prepared by rehearsing a hypothetical conversation. "If she says… Then I'll say…"

I was stopped mid-sentence by a twinge of conviction. I knew getting myself worked up over pretend insults was not God's best for me. The Spirit nudged. Rather than preparing my comeback, I should have been preparing my heart. I immediately stopped to pray.

Look, it's not wrong to be ready in advance by knowing healthy responses to use when conflict arises. But that's not what I was doing. At that moment, I was trying to come up with the perfect zinger so I could have the last word. When faced with the risk of an uncomfortable interaction, it's easy to get caught up in imaginary arguments. We must remember that rather than attempt to script every scenario that may play out, it is far more effective to prepare our hearts.

For all of those stressful Christmases—even with the unrelenting preparation of food and gifts and decorations—I was still ambushed when the day arrived. My heart wasn't prepared for exhaustion, for conflict, for disappointment, for the unexpected.

On "Our First Best Christmas," the changes made were more than a shift in activity. Preparing my heart was instrumental in cultivating a restful season. The world's pattern causes us to be caught off-guard by the stress of the holidays. A prepared heart comes from the working of a renewed mind.

### What does it look like to Prepare Your Heart?

To *Prepare Your Heart* is a cultivating work that happens on the inside before it develops in our activities. As you heard from my cautionary tale above, it is not best to wait until minutes before our celebrations to start preparing our hearts for Christmas. The meaning of the word *prepare* is to *get ready before*. This is a job to be done in advance.

INTERNAL EXAMINATION:
***Ask.** "You do not have because you do not ask God." That truth, from James 4:2, is not an invitation to view God like Santa Claus and expect Him to fulfill our Christmas wishlist. The context of this verse reminds us not to try to make things happen on our own and not to ask God with wrong motives. But, if we desire to cultivate a restful season, we need to ask God. The prayers at the end of each chapter are designed to help us do this, and we will continue to talk about the power of our *ask* in the chapters ahead.

# Way 3- You: Prepare Your Heart

Preparing our hearts is something we cannot do on our own. But the good news is, when we ask, God will answer. Ask God to prepare your heart.

"If any of you lacks wisdom, you should ask God, who gives generously to all without finding fault, and it will be given to you. But when you ask, you must believe and not doubt, because the one who doubts is like a wave of the sea, blown and tossed by the wind. That person should not expect to receive anything from the Lord." James 1:5-7

We need wisdom. It's something we should specifically ask for as we navigate the holiday season. James not only tells us that we should ask, but he also addresses the posture of our hearts as we inquire of God. The truth applies as we ask for wisdom, and as we ask God to prepare our hearts. We must believe and not doubt. When we ask, it is with expectation, anticipating that God will do what we have asked Him to do according to His will.

"This is the confidence we have in approaching God: that if we ask anything according to his will, he hears us." 1 John 5:14

***Examine your heart.** Preparing our hearts for Christmas involves honest self-evaluation, examining our thoughts and attitudes and actions. We need to understand our own role in the stress of Christmases past so we can address those issues.

We have been using the word *cultivate* to convey *development* or *improvement*. But *cultivate* also means to prepare land for growing crops. Scripture often uses ancient agricultural references to teach us spiritual lessons. These illustrations resonate with me as my family tends to our microfarm. In biblical analogies, our hearts are often compared to the ground. Preparing earth for planting means pulling weeds and breaking up the soil. Preparing our hearts looks similar.

# 12 Ways of Christmas

Weeds represent the things that don't belong in our lives. Things we have allowed to grow and take root. They crowd out the desired crop and rob it of nutrients. Nothing good grows in hard soil or in a hard heart. This callousness of the soul is the result of rebellion and unrepentant sin. A prepared heart is soft and ready to receive.

We talked in the last chapter about loving others well by asking good questions. We can love ourselves and get ready for Christmas in the same way, by taking a deep introspective look. The list below will deal specifically with our own internal issues. (We'll get to the external stuff next.)

What fear or anxiety is crowding out the good things in my heart and stealing my energy?

Are there emotional, mental, and spiritual weeds that need to be removed from my life?

What do I need to work through before the holidays arrive?

Am I harboring hidden sin that requires confession and repentance?

Have I hardened my heart with bitterness or unforgiveness that will get in the way of a restful season?

Include God in your self-examination. Ask Him to reveal the areas of your heart that need to be addressed. This passage from the Psalms can become a prayer of reflection:

> *"Search me, God, and know my heart;*
> *test me and know my anxious thoughts.*
> *See if there is any offensive way in me,*
> *and lead me in the way everlasting."*
> Psalm 139:23-24

**\*Surrender.** Asking God to prepare our hearts and making honest personal observations is the easy part. Identifying the weeds and hard-heartedness is one thing, but dealing with them is quite another. Recognizing our need to

## Way 3- You: Prepare Your Heart

forgive is the first step, but extending forgiveness is a journey. Admitting our sin is the beginning, but true repentance means expressing sincere remorse and making a commitment to turn away from that sin. The real challenge is surrendering to the work God wants to do.

Surrender. That is a hard word. Letting go reminds us that we are not in control and loosening our grip somehow feels like losing. But surrendering to God does not make us prisoners; it sets us free. We need the freedom that only Jesus can bring—freedom from the weeds and hard soil—in order to flourish in the abundance God has for us.

If you're a doer like me, you like the idea of having some action items. I thrive on practical application. But the *12 Ways* are more complex than a change in our activity. Our behaviors will change as the result of a transformed heart through a renewed mind. Heart change is something the Holy Spirit produces in us. He does not leave us to do the work on our own, but He also will not do all the work for us. Jesus calls us His co-laborers. That applies to Kingdom work and the work to be done in our own lives. Life change is a collaboration, partnering with God in a cooperative process.

As you consider the issues identified in the previous section you have to do the groundwork (pun totally intended), and surrender to the Holy Spirit in making the appropriate changes.

PROCESS EXTERNAL STRESSORS:

We know we cannot wait until Christmas arrives to prepare our hearts. But there is another, opposite and equally unhealthy way to deal with our issues—obsession—milling the problems over and over from Thanksgiving to New Year. There is a balance between avoiding and obsessing. Before the holidays arrive, we need to confront what causes us stress.

Preparing your heart is more than getting in the mood or catching the Christmas spirit. Processing your stressors is about loving yourself the way God loves you. You need to

# 12 Ways of Christmas

remember that you have been bought with a price. Jesus came to give you abundant life in Him. You are worth the effort to recognize and address what has not been working for you during the holidays.

***Make a list.** If you look at the sides of my refrigerator or the stack of papers next to my laptop, you'll find more than a few lists. Taking an inventory in this way helps me to untangle my thoughts and keep things in order. At Christmas, making to-do lists and to-buy lists and to-bring lists keeps my life and mind organized, and those kinds of lists may help you, too. But since we're talking about preparing our hearts, the list we want to make will enumerate what keeps us from a restful season. This is not a problem-solving activity. For now, we are identifying our concerns.

What are you anxious or worried about?
What has been a source of disappointment in previous years?
What activities and situations have you stressed out about the holidays?

***Journal.** What emotions come up when you consider the stressors on your list? Journaling in real life doesn't have to be reminiscent of the heroine in a dreamy vintage novel. You don't have to write a memoir to be held in posterity for generations to come. Unless you want to. Journaling can look however feels right to you. The purpose is to have a creative outlet to process your thoughts and feelings.

I have several different journals for different applications, but I don't personally keep what would be considered a diary. I cannot retain a record of every idea that pops into my head; some thoughts are keepers, and others are not. Writing is the way I process the world. So, for me, journaling to process looks more like scribbling down what's in my head on whatever paper is handy. I'm not worried about grammar,

## Way 3- You: Prepare Your Heart

usage, and punctuation. I'm concerned about articulating my thoughts and feelings so they are no longer bouncing around in my head unexpressed. Once I have processed my feelings, I don't need to hold onto the paper anymore—they are free to be released into the universe or the woodstove.

***Have a conversation.** I am an external processor. That means if I have not worked through my issues, they just come out, unfiltered, sometimes in uncomfortable and embarrassing situations.

Talking it out does not look like blabbing your issues on social media or ranting to anyone who will listen. We all have those friends who we know will tell us what we want to hear, but we need someone who will speak the truth in love rather than commiserate. Share what you are processing with your spouse, a trusted friend, a spiritual advisor, or a professional counselor. This person should be a Christ-follower, mature and godly, who will point you to Scripture over their own opinion.

God places people in our lives to come alongside us in our journey, people who are there for comfort and support and wise counsel. But these relationships are meant to be in addition to, not instead of, talking to Him. There are times when I prayed for God to prepare my heart, but I did not let Him in and involve Him in the process. When addressing the concerns that cause us stress at Christmas, the most important conversation we should have is with God.

The prophet Isaiah said Jesus would be called Wonderful Counselor (9:6). Jesus possesses all of the knowledge and wisdom we need for the abundant life God intended. He is qualified to direct us as we seek His wise counsel.

In John 14:16, Jesus told His disciples that after He left earth, the Father would send another Advocate (NIV), Helper (ESV), Comforter (KJV), Counselor (CSB) "to help you and be with you forever." This is the promised Holy Spirit, who takes up residence in us when we receive Jesus as our Savior. Among the many spiritual blessing the Holy Spirit brings, He is an ever-present guide as we navigate the difficulties in our lives.

First Peter 5:7 says, "Cast all your anxiety on him because he cares for you." This verse invites us to take the heavy load we've been carrying and toss it off onto Him. Jesus loves you. He cares for you. What matters to you matters to Him. He can be trusted. The culmination of talking to God about our concerns is surrendering them to Him. As we release our burdens and hand them over to Jesus, we experience a lifting of the weight we tried to carry alone.

**\*Take heart.** Many of the strategies in this book will help to reduce the stressors we're addressing. I am, by nature, a problem solver. So I want to start fixing issues before I even get to the root cause. The purpose of processing our stressors is not to eliminate all of them.

Jesus said, "In this world you will have trouble." Of all the Bible promises, I have never seen this one ironed onto a T-shirt. But that promise, as unsettling as it may seem, comes glued to the invitation to "take heart" and the truth that Jesus "has overcome the world." (John 16:33)

No matter how much work we put in, no matter how fully we surrender, we will never entirely rid our holidays of struggle. As long as we remain on this earth, we will keep having problems. But we can be bolstered by the hope that they will not overtake us because our Jesus has overcome the world.

The truth is, sometimes God changes our circumstances, but other times He changes us through our circumstances. Externally, life may not look much different, but the way we approach it can. Our hearts can be prepared to deal with challenges in a way that honors God and is respectful to others.

# Way 3- You: Prepare Your Heart

## Dual Purpose

When we moved to our little log cabin on the creek a few years ago, some stuff had to go. Our home doesn't quite qualify as a tiny house, but it's about half the size of the place we lived before. Due to space constraints, we no longer have room for uni-taskers, you know, tools and kitchen appliances that serve a single purpose like the bread maker and sno-cone machine.

One of the dynamic things about the *12 Ways* is that, to some degree, each one has more than one purpose in our lives. Everything we do to love God with all of our being compels us to love others well and enables us to love ourselves in a balanced way. When we put others' needs above our own, it honors God, and we are blessed in the process. When we learn to care for ourselves, we are more able to genuinely love God and love others.

There's an example of a dual-purpose principle in the last chapter, where we discussed being present as a practical way to put others first. The mutual benefit of being present is that we also enjoy connection and making memories.

Many of the principles we learn in other chapters will also contribute to preparing our hearts for Christmas. For instance, let's look at worship. Worship is 100% about God and 0% about us, otherwise, it isn't really worship at all. But our God is so gracious that in the very act of bringing Him glory, we are transformed. While God is the purpose and the center, worship also prepares our hearts by shifting our focus from ourselves and our circumstances. It places our full attention on Jesus.

As we learn to choose joy and pursue peace and find rest, we will see that these, too, are mechanisms for preparing our hearts. Keep a lookout for these dual-purpose principles. I may point out a few of them, but it will also be exciting for you to discover them for yourself.

# 12 Ways of Christmas

As we identify our internal and external stressors, may we surrender to the work God wants to do in our lives and cast our cares on Him. Let's partner with Jesus to prepare our hearts for the season ahead.

**PRAY:**
*Thank You, Lord, for prescribing celebration by setting aside holy days that we may honor You. Examine me, show me what changes need to be made in my life, and help me to surrender to the work You want to do. Allow me to process those things that would bring stress during the holidays and teach me to trust You with them. Amongst all the preparations for this Christmas, please help me most of all to prepare my heart. In Jesus' name, amen.*

**MEDITATE OR MEMORIZE:**
"This is the confidence we have in approaching God: that if we ask anything according to his will, he hears us." 1 John 5:14

"Search me, God, and know my heart; test me and know my anxious thoughts. See if there is any offensive way in me, and lead me in the way everlasting." Psalm 139:23-24

"Cast all your anxiety on him because he cares for you." 1 Peter 5:7

**CONSIDER:**
1. Share some practical ways you can transform the holidays back into holy days that are honoring to God.

# Way 3- You: Prepare Your Heart

2. What has been your experience with having an unprepared heart at Christmas?

3. How were you challenged in considering your own role in a stressful Christmas by asking God to prepare your heart, examining your heart, and surrendering to the work God wants to do?

4. As you process external stressors, which method is most effective for you? Is it to make a list, journal, have a conversation, or something else? Why?

5. Respond to the truth, "Sometimes God changes our circumstances, but other times He changes us through our circumstances."

# Way 4- Jesus:

# Seek Him

"After Jesus was born in Bethlehem in Judea, during the time of King Herod, Magi from the east came to Jerusalem and asked, 'Where is the one who has been born king of the Jews? We saw his star when it rose and have come to worship him.'

When King Herod heard this he was disturbed, and all Jerusalem with him. When he had called together all the people's chief priests and teachers of the law, he asked them where the Messiah was to be born. 'In Bethlehem in Judea,' they replied, 'for this is what the prophet has written:

"But you, Bethlehem, in the land of Judah,
are by no means least among the rulers of Judah;
for out of you will come a ruler
who will shepherd my people Israel."'

Then Herod called the Magi secretly and found out from them the exact time the star had appeared. He sent them to Bethlehem and said, 'Go and search carefully for the child. As soon as you find him, report to me, so that I too may go and worship him.'

After they had heard the king, they went on their way, and the star they had seen when it rose went ahead of them until it stopped over the place where the child was." Matthew 2:1-9

# 12 Ways of Christmas

The Magi, who we traditionally call the wise men, set out on a journey from far off to find Jesus. This is a pretty commonly known element of the Christmas story. But, their visit did not occur quite the way our table-top Nativity sets might lead us to believe. The wise men were not present at the manger scene in Bethlehem. "His star" appeared at the time of Jesus' birth. The Magi saw the star, but not just with their eyes. The word used here indicates they saw spiritually. They recognized that this was no ordinary star through spiritual discernment. The star was a birth announcement, an exclamation of the Messiah's arrival. Upon observing the sign, they were compelled to seek Him.

The wise men asked, "Where is the one who has been born the king of the Jews?" They had journeyed to find the One and only, the King of kings. That's who we need to pursue this Christmas. Rather than be consumed by all the trimmings, hoping they will finally fill our longing for the perfect holiday, we need to seek the only One who will satisfy.

The Messiah has arrived! The good news is that we don't have to travel far like the wise men did. Acts 17:27 tells us, "God did this so that they would seek him and perhaps reach out for him and find him, though he is not far from any one of us."

When we seek Him, we will find Him. When we draw near to God, He draws near to us. When we go after His presence, God blesses us with communion.

Where the passage above reads, "We have come to worship him," *The Message* Bible paraphrase uses these words, "We are on a pilgrimage to worship Him." The word *pilgrimage* means *a journey to a holy place*. The mission of the Magi was to find and worship Jesus.

God is so vast and so dynamic. Like the wise men, we require spiritual discernment to even begin to understand Him. After we have given our lives to Jesus, we will spend the rest of our days on this earth getting to know Him, growing in

# Way 4- Jesus: Seek Him

relationship with Him, and being transformed to look more like Him. Seeking Jesus is not a destination; it is a pilgrimage—an ongoing journey to a holy place.

**Searching**

My heart skipped a beat as my left thumb traced a vacant space on the third finger. I looked down reluctantly, hoping my eyes wouldn't see what my heart already knew to be true—my ring finger was bare. A scene ensued as I frantically flailed my hands shouting across the store to Chris. The custom-designed engagement ring he had given me just a few weeks earlier had somehow slipped from my finger and was nowhere to be found. If this happened today, after over two decades of marriage to this man, I wouldn't have been so nervous. But I was unsure of how my, then, fiancé might react. Chris looked at me calmly, shook his head, and immediately joined in my search, scanning back and forth, studying every square inch of the floor. We retraced my steps, canvassing every aisle. Eventually, the gold band was found beneath a garment rack. I slid the ring back on my finger and held my hand out admiring the glistening diamond as if it were the first moment I had seen it. Chris smiled, shaking his head again.

At that moment, we weren't worried about what we were having for dinner or who we would be hanging out with the next day. The only thing that mattered right then was finding my ring, and we did not stop looking until it was found. And that is the same fervor with which we need to seek Jesus.

"So do not worry, saying, 'What shall we eat?' or 'What shall we drink?' or 'What shall we wear?' For the pagans run after all these things, and your heavenly Father knows that you need them. But seek first his kingdom and his righteousness, and all these things will be given to you as well."
Matthew 6:31-33

# 12 Ways of Christmas

Could Jesus have spoken more directly to the heart of all my stressful Christmases? Some years I left Him out altogether with barely an acknowledgment. But other times, like Martha, I made room for Jesus and invited Him in, but I was too busy to spend time with Him. I was "worried about many things" like what we were going to eat and drink and wear, instead of giving my full attention to the one thing that matters most.

God knows all of our needs, and He does not ask us to deny them. Instead, He invites us to seek relationship with Him first and trust Him to provide all these things. The world's pattern for Christmas is to go after our own self-fulfillment; a renewed mind is set on seeking Jesus.

## What does it look like to Seek Him?

To *Seek Him* means to search out God's presence and strive after relationship with Him. Scripture describes the sincerity and intensity with which we are to seek Him.

Seek Him with all your heart. (Deuteronomy 4:29, Psalm 119:2, Jeremiah 29:13)
Seek Him with all your soul. (Deuteronomy 4:29)
Seek His face always. (1 Chronicles 16:11, Psalm 105:4)
Seek Him earnestly. (Psalm 63:1, Hebrews 11:6)

We are going to look at what it means to seek God in Prayer, in His Word, and in Community. These spiritual disciplines are not religious rituals; they are relationship builders.

SEEK HIM IN PRAYER:
Simplistically, prayer is a conversation with God, but the many aspects of prayer are complex.

# Way 4- Jesus: Seek Him

***Road trip.** My friend Pam and I loaded up her minivan with two teenage boys, one rambunctious golden doodle, and enough snacks to last a month. (Ahem. Or two days for the aforementioned teenage boys.) We headed out on a road trip to visit our friend Sara and her kiddos. What if I woke up in the morning, thanked Sara for breakfast and checked the itinerary for the day, then told her I needed a fresh towel and didn't talk to either of them the rest of the day? Of course, that didn't happen. The days were full of laughter and conversation—about everything. We talked about our kids and the weather and the food we were eating and the places we were walking. I was constantly aware that I was there with my friends. I didn't even have to be intentional to engage with them. The reason we made the trip was to spend time together.

We know we don't have to travel far to find Jesus when we sincerely seek Him. Jesus came from Heaven to earth to be ever-present with us on our pilgrimage. Because He is Immanuel, God with us, He is by our side every step of the journey. The Christian life is like being on a road trip with Jesus as we learn to live and love like He does. Our conversations with Him shouldn't be limited to a 10-minute window in the morning. We need connection with Him all day, every day, throughout the day. We can invite Him in during all of our activities by talking to Him while shopping and wrapping and baking and decorating. Our every moment can be a God-included moment when we remain aware of His presence and continually turn our hearts to Him.

In 1 Thessalonians 5:17, Paul wrote, "Pray without ceasing." I'm no Greek scholar or any other scholar for that matter, but I came across this in my Bible study. The word translated *without ceasing* is a Greek term used to describe a hacking cough or anything recurring constantly. Think about that! When you have a severe cold, coughing isn't something you consciously think about. It's a reflex.

# 12 Ways of Christmas

How would our spiritual lives change if talking to God about every single thing just became so natural that we didn't even have to think about it? If prayer became a reflex? Every worry, every concern, every unexpected blessing can become like a tickle in our throat, a cue to pray.

***Two-way conversation.** Just like leaning into relationship with our friends and family, including God in our activities is good. But being present with Jesus also means we show Him value through dedicated time when we give Him our undivided attention.

Like in most of my interactions with others, I have had a real tendency to monopolize the conversation with God. I often spend my entire prayer time talking about me. I go over my schedule for the day, externally process my concerns, and offer up the wish list. In a way, I reduced God to a personal assistant or sounding board. As we said before, Jesus is called Wonderful Counselor, and talking to Him should include, but not be limited to processing my own thoughts and feelings.

A one-sided conversation is actually more of a monologue. That's cool for the start of a talk show, but not so much for building a relationship. So often, we wonder why we are not hearing from God. Meanwhile, we're doing all of the talking and not giving Him space to speak. Conversation with God means that occasionally we need to shut the cake-hole (Did you forget? Always cake.) and let Him get a word in.

Being with Jesus is not all about what He can do for me. In fact, so much more so, our relationship is about how I can bring Him glory. Like Martha's sister Mary, Jesus invites us to choose what is better by sitting at His feet and listening.

SEEK HIM IN HIS WORD:
God speaks to us through His Word. It's easy to go through the motions of reading the Bible in order to check it off the list. But as our minds are renewed, we learn to read Scripture

## Way 4- Jesus: Seek Him

with the expectation to hear from God and with the intention to obey what He says.

For years I felt guilty when I heard women at church talk about the importance of their early morning "quiet time." I'm not much of a morning person. Back then, I was getting up at 5:45 am, rushing around to get my son dressed and fed and taken to childcare before hurrying to work and running in the door at the last minute. I tried to get up earlier to study my Bible, but even when I didn't fall back to sleep, I couldn't remember what I had read because my brain wasn't awake yet. I often say, "God wants out firstfruits not our leftovers." This is great direction for giving God the best of our monetary and material assets. However, this concept also applies to giving God the best of our time and attention. Our study of God's Word doesn't have to be first thing in the morning; it needs to be the part of the day when we are most alert, undistracted, and able to focus on what He is saying to us.

I've never been able to stick with a routine, probably because I like variety, so I switch up my method of Bible study frequently. As we unpack ways to engage with Scripture, I present many different options to try, but this is not a suggestion to fit each practice into every day. Choose one or two that suits you.

**\*Start small and stay the course.** If you have never established a rhythm of Bible study, don't be overwhelmed by the idea of adding one more thing to your holiday to-do list. Zechariah 4:10 reminds us not to be ashamed of small beginnings. A small beginning could look like downloading a Bible app, getting a push-notification for the verse of the day, or a daily devotion sent to your inbox. Whatever small step you take, know it doesn't have to be perfect to be progress. Every moment of seeking God in His Word is a move forward.

For those who already practice regular study, the noise of Christmas can sometimes distract us from our normal habits. When our schedules become more full and our small groups take a break from formal study, we still need to meet with Jesus daily. I want to encourage you to stay the course. Remain dedicated to leaning into relationship with God through time in His Word throughout the holiday season.

**\*Look for yourself.** There is an endless supply of Bible study resources and daily devotionals of which I am an avid consumer. I want to read and learn everything I can to grow in my walk with Jesus. So, I want to encourage you to use these tools as well.

God so often teaches us through the insights and experiences of others. But He also wants to speak to you directly through His Word, not solely through someone else who has read His Word. Just like giving our undivided attention to one-on-one conversation with God, our Bible study needs to include time when there are no other voices but His. We hear Him as we read for ourselves what He is saying.

You know, there was a time when the Scriptures were not attainable for the common people. Today, we have unprecedented access to the Bible, and we must not take that for granted. God's Word has been translated into thousands of languages and is available in numerous easy-to-read translations. You can read the Bible in print, online, and there's even an app for that.

From Genesis to Revelation and every word in between, the whole of Scripture is His story. God promises that His Word will not return void, so anywhere you read in the Bible is a good place to be. But in December, I like to focus at least some of my Bible study on connecting with the true meaning of Christmas by reading the passages about Jesus' birth.

**\*Meditate:** Mary, mother of Jesus, experienced miracle after miracle leading up to His birth. Luke 2:19 says, "But Mary treasured up all these things and pondered them in her heart."

# Way 4- Jesus: Seek Him

Mary may not have understood everything God was doing at the time, but she held close the things she had seen and heard. That is how I want to handle Scripture. I don't always understand what I read, but rather than moving on, I desire to treasure up His Word and ponder it in my heart.

"Keep this Book of the Law always on your lips; meditate on it day and night, so that you may be careful to do everything written in it. Then you will be prosperous and successful." Joshua 1:8

Meditate on God's Word by keeping it in front of you and storing it in your heart. Write a verse on a notecard and post it where you're likely to see it. Recite a passage out loud or commit it to memory. Incorporate Scripture in your décor. (I think this calls for a trip to Hobby Lobby!)

One of my favorite ways to ponder is to write Scripture. This activity helps to slow down my mind and also to engage different parts of my brain in the process. I have a journal dedicated to Scripture writing and a chart listing every book in the Bible so I can mark them off as I go. During the holidays, I put this into practice by writing the Christmas story passages from Matthew and Luke.

SEEK HIM IN COMMUNITY:

At Christmas with all the activities and getting together with family and friends, we must not forget to make room to gather in Christian community. "And let us not neglect our meeting together, as some people do, but encourage one another, especially now that the day of his return is drawing near." Hebrews 10:25 (NLT)

I'll never stop saying this: we are better together. God designed us to live and learn and worship and grow in relationship with other believers. Christian community looks like Matthew 18:20, "For where two or three are gathered in my name, there I am with them." When we come together with our brothers and sisters in Christ for the purpose of seeking God, He is present. The value of community is so dual-purpose that it would be difficult to say that it benefits one area more than the others. We need each other. Community encourages us personally and builds up the people who we come together with, and it is also honoring to God. Together is a place where we not only grow closer to each other but closer to Him.

### Shema

Our key passage, presented clear back in the first chapter—the one that tells us to love God with all of our being and love our neighbor as ourselves—starts out this way, "Hear, O Israel, the Lord our God, the Lord is one." For generations, these verses have been a prayer the Jewish people repeat every morning and evening. The prayer is called *The Shema* because *shema* is the Hebrew word we see translated as *hear*, but it has a deeper meaning than to just listen with our physical ears. The greatest commandment begins by telling us to *shema*—pay attention to what is said, and act upon what we hear by behaving differently. This truth is echoed in the book of James when he exhorts us to be not only hearers of the Word but doers also.

We hear from God as we seek Him in prayer, in His Word, and in community. As we listen, let's intently *shema*—learn and live what He speaks. Our minds are renewed, and our lives are transformed as we actively live a lifestyle of seeking Him.

**PRAY:**
*Dear God, may all my days be marked by a pilgrimage to grow in relationship with You. Teach me to seek You with all my heart and find You. Speak to me as I come to You in prayer, engage with Your Word, and connect in community. Help me to not only listen to what You say but to be transformed as I obey You. In Jesus' name, amen.*

# Way 4- Jesus: Seek Him

**MEDITATE OR MEMORIZE:**
"God did this so that they would seek him and perhaps reach out for him and find him, though he is not far from any one of us." Acts 17:27

"So do not worry, saying, 'What shall we eat?' or 'What shall we drink?' or 'What shall we wear?' For the pagans run after all these things, and your heavenly Father knows that you need them. But seek first his kingdom and his righteousness, and all these things will be given to you as well." Matthew 6:31-33

"You will seek me find me when you seek me with all your heart." Jeremiah 29:13

**CONSIDER:**
1. "The Christian life is like a road trip with Jesus." How can you make every moment a God-included moment throughout the holiday season?

2. Have your conversations with God been more of a monologue? How will you give space for Him to speak?

3. Describe your next step to seek God in His Word—start small, stay the course, look for yourself, or meditate.

4. What does it mean for you to seek Jesus in community?

5. What would it look like for you to *shema*—listen and act upon what you hear—this Christmas?

# WAY 5- Others:

# Spread the Word

"And there were shepherds living out in the fields nearby, keeping watch over their flocks at night. An angel of the Lord appeared to them, and the glory of the Lord shone around them, and they were terrified. But the angel said to them, 'Do not be afraid. I bring you good news that will cause great joy for all the people. Today in the town of David a Savior has been born to you; he is the Messiah, the Lord. This will be a sign to you: You will find a baby wrapped in cloths and lying in a manger.'

Suddenly a great company of the heavenly host appeared with the angel, praising God and saying, 'Glory to God in the highest heaven, and on earth peace to those on whom his favor rests.'

When the angels had left them and gone into heaven, the shepherds said to one another, 'Let's go to Bethlehem and see this thing that has happened, which the Lord has told us about.'

So they hurried off and found Mary and Joseph, and the baby, who was lying in the manger. When they had seen him, they spread the word concerning what had been told them about this child, and all who heard it were amazed at what the shepherds said to them." Luke 2:8-18

# 12 Ways of Christmas

One of my favorite Christmas traditions is gathering in the living room with my family to watch "A Charlie Brown Christmas." And, by far, the best part of the show is when Charlie Brown cries out in frustration, "Isn't there anyone who knows what Christmas is all about?" Then Linus (the kid who always carries around a blue blanket) recites the first part of the passage above. "That's what Christmas is all about, Charlie Brown."[1]

The shepherds were not Bible scholars who knew all the deep theological answers. But, oh, they could not keep to themselves what they had seen and heard! And, just like them, we don't need to have all the answers. We just have to be willing to share our own stories about how we have experienced Jesus, and what He has done in our lives. That is what Christmas is all about!

When the shepherds heard the good news, they did not deliberate over whether they should go. They didn't play rock/paper/scissors to decide who would stay with the sheep. In fact, *The Message* records Luke 2:15a-16 this way, "'Let's get over to Bethlehem as fast as we can and see for ourselves what God has revealed to us.' They left, running, and found Mary and Joseph, and the baby lying in the manger." The shepherds left everything behind. They didn't walk; they ran to see the Messiah.

After experiencing Jesus, the shepherds did not hurry back to their flocks, which were also their livelihood. "They spread the word," (NIV) "made widely known," (NKJV) "told everyone they met," (MSG) "spread the story," (VOICE) "publicized widely," (WEB) "what had been told to them about the child." (NIV)

We cannot keep the message of Christmas to ourselves! We previously talked about inviting Jesus in, making room for

---

[1] *A Charlie Brown Christmas*. Bill Melendez. Lee Mendelson Films, 1965.

# Way 5- Others: Spread the Word

Him during the holidays. We put Jesus first in our own hearts by including Him, and also by pointing others to Him. Spreading the Word is not only a way to make Jesus the center, it is also a way to love others well. Caring for the spiritual needs of our family and friends means sharing the true meaning of Christmas. The world's customs leave Jesus out of the message of Christmas. A renewed mind knows our purpose is to know God and to make Him known.

In our celebration of Christmas, we often focus on the nativity scene. This is the beautiful moment when the Creator of the universe, who took on human flesh to become one of us, entered the world. But Christmas isn't just about a moment, it's about a movement. There's more to the story than Jesus being born. Our pilgrimage doesn't end in Bethlehem; the manger is only the beginning that leads us to the cross.

After Jesus' death and resurrection, before returning to Heaven, He had some parting words for His followers.

"Therefore go and make disciples of all nations, baptizing them in the name of the Father and of the Son and of the Holy Spirit, and teaching them to obey everything I have commanded you. And surely I am with you always, to the very end of the age." Matthew 28:19-20

These verses above are known as The Great Commission. Now, think back to our key verse. Remember, The Greatest Commandment? Do you see how these two things fit together? In this chapter, we are focusing on the part of the Greatest Commandment that tells us to love our neighbor. When we love others well, we want the best for them, God's best for them, which is relationship with Jesus. When we have experienced Jesus, we will want others to experience Him, too. Found people want others to be found.

**The Greatest Commandment is fulfilled in the Great Commission.** "Love your neighbor as yourself" is carried out when we spread the word, sharing the good news about Jesus with others.

# 12 Ways of Christmas

## Christmas Service

When I was a little girl, I knew my grandparents were not believers. In my childish misunderstanding, that was true because they did not do all the good things Christians are supposed to do, and they did a lot of the bad things we were not allowed to do. I was afraid Grandma and Grandpa would die and go to hell. But every year on the Sunday closest to Christmas, they joined us for a special church service. My family put on their Sunday best. I bounced through the door in my fluffy holiday dress and slippery church shoes, Grandpa Red wore the three-piece suit and tie which were usually reserved for weddings and funerals, and Grandma Phyllis glided in wearing high-heals and a fur coat. For that one night, I was filled with excitement hoping it would be the day for my grandparents to get saved.

Listen, I now understand that we are saved by grace through faith and not by works (Ephesians 2:8-9). A legalistic list of rules does not determine anyone's eternity. When we accept Jesus as our Savior, the Holy Spirit takes up residence on the inside, and God starts to change us. He wants to make us holy so we look more like Jesus. That may include addressing some of our habits and hang-ups. But our Father always changes us from the inside out. God is not interested in behavior modification; He is all about life transformation through relationship with Him.

My Grandpa Red was in his 70's when he received Jesus as His Savior just days before he went home to be with Him. Soon after Grandpa had passed, Grandma Phyllis gave her life to Jesus and lived many more years serving Him. We will never know what seeds were planted throughout their decades of life or which of those seeds finally sprouted into relationship with Jesus. But perhaps hearing the gospel presented once every year when they attended church for Christmas made a difference in their hearts.

# Way 5- Others: Spread the Word

**What does it look like to Spread the Word to Others?**

To *Spread the Word* means to share Jesus with others. Jesus is relational. When we have experienced relationship with Him, we are commissioned to point other people to the same relationship.

When we decide to look at the Christmas story in Scripture, we don't generally think to turn to the Gospel of John. Now, John does not tell us about encounters with Joseph and the wise men like we read in Matthew, nor does he share the narrative of Mary and the shepherds like in the Gospel of Luke. But John does, in fact, have something to say about Jesus' birth story.

John 1:14 says, "The Word became flesh and made his dwelling among us. We have seen his glory, the glory of the one and only Son, who came from the Father, full of grace and truth."

John used the Greek word *logos,* translated as *Word,* in referring to Jesus. HELPS Word-studies explains *logos* this way: "a common term for a person sharing a message," or "expressing the thoughts of the Father through the Spirit."[2] You see, in telling the good news about Jesus, we are, in effect, spreading the Word Himself.

Look, I know I'm not the only one who squirms in my seat a little when people start talking about sharing the gospel. We love Jesus, and we want the people we care about to know His love. But figuring out how to share our faith can be scary. However, we can have confidence knowing that through the Holy Spirit, the Father will give us the ability to express His thoughts to share His message.

---

[2] HELPS Word-studies, Copyright © 1987, 2011 by Helps Ministries, Inc.

# 12 Ways of Christmas

EXTEND AN INVITATION:

**\*Invite Jesus in.** Making room for Jesus by including Him in our holidays has a dual purpose. When we invite Him into our celebrations, others who don't know Him will see a glimpse of who He is. Sharing your faith does not have to be overt or complicated. You can start small with the things you are already doing.

I told you before, one of the ways we make room in our celebrations is with our traditional birthday cake for Jesus. (Have I mentioned cake much?) Honoring Him in this way is also a witness to the person at the bakery when I place my order and ask them to write "Happy Birthday, Jesus" in red icing. This same cake also plants seeds about the true meaning of Christmas for anyone in my family who hasn't made the decision to follow Jesus.

Your Christmas cards and decorations and background music and social media posts can all serve as vehicles to spread the Word and point people to Jesus.

**\*Invite others to come see.** According to LifeWay Research, 61% of Americans typically attend church at Christmas. Of those who don't, 57% say they would likely attend if someone they knew invited them.[3]

We know going to church does not automatically make our loved ones saved. But only God knows the seeds that are planted by extending the invitation, whether it is accepted or not.

Asking our friends and family to join us for church is not about attending a service or event together. We are extending an invitation for them to come see for themselves and experience who Jesus is. This is an invitation to listen as we pray and have one-on-one communication with God, to hear His Word where He reveals Himself to us, and to fellowship

---

[3] Carol Pipes, *No Place Like Church for the Holidays*, LifeWay Research, December 14, 2015, https://lifewayresearch.com/2015/12/14/ no-place-like-church-for-the-holidays/

# Way 5- Others: Spread the Word

in our community of believers. As others observe and participate in seeking Him, we hope they will find Him.

HAVE AN ANSWER:

Colossians 4:5-6 says, "Be wise in the way you act toward outsiders; make the most of every opportunity. Let your conversation be always with grace, seasoned with salt, so that you may know how to answer everyone."

Spreading the Word about Jesus does not have to be forced or pushy. If we are willing to sharing the gospel, God will present us with opportunities. The Holy Spirit will prompt us; conversations will organically move to the topic of faith. And Paul encourages us to be wise and make the most of those opportunities by being full of grace and knowing how to answer.

I love how this Colossians verse parallels what we read earlier in John 1:14 saying Jesus was full of both grace and truth. I don't have a hard time telling the truth, but I often forget to give grace as I'm doing so. I think most of us err on one side or the other. We can look to Jesus' perfect example of balancing both when we spread the Word. We can tell others the truth about their need for a Savior while at the same time extending the grace He has given us.

Now, I'm no good at knowing what to say off-the-cuff. I love to speak in front of an audience of any size when I'm prepared. But interviews always make me especially nervous because I prefer to know in advance what I want to say. When we share the good news of Jesus with others, it's kind of like an interview situation. We cannot know every question that will come up or where the conversation will lead. And while we can't possibly have all the answers, we can make an effort to prepare. Consider in advance what you might say if someone asks you about your relationship with Jesus, and be ready to explain how they can have what you have.

# 12 Ways of Christmas

***Invite others into your story.** You might be feeling like you're not qualified to share the gospel or maybe you don't know what to say. I get it. I was terrified to write the chapter in my book, *Make Me a Blessing,* about how we bless others by sharing Jesus. I did not have a lot of experience in what I thought would count as witnessing, and I had no idea what to talk about. But God showed me a truth that is probably true for you too. I was already spreading the Word in more ways than I realized, and if I would be surrendered to be used by Him, He would give me more opportunities and equip me to share.

Look, in Jesus' time, shepherds were considered to have the lowest of professions. These men would have been seen as unclean, uneducated, and the most unexpected messengers of God's Word. But God uses whoever He chooses to spread His truth. The shepherds were eyewitnesses to the promised Messiah. They did not have to make a formal speech or memorize a pitch. They simply gave testimony to all they had seen and heard.

People are more compelled by real-life experiences than a theoretical anecdote about what Jesus could do for someone. You are living proof that Jesus changes lives today, and your story matters. Your first-hand, eyewitness account of new life in Christ is a credible testimony.

These 3 questions will help you to get started as you consider how to share your own faith story:

What was my life like before Jesus?
How did I come to receive Him as my Savior?
How has my life changed in relationship with Jesus?

"In the same way, let your light shine before others, that they may see your good deeds and glorify your Father in heaven." Matthew 5:16

# Way 5- Others: Spread the Word

A lifestyle of putting Jesus first and putting others' needs above your own is counter-cultural. Beyond using your words to share your story, the best testimony is when you invite others into your life and they observe you living in a way that reflects Jesus.

***Invite others to receive.** In *Way 1: Make Room,* I spoke directly to unbelievers about what starting a relationship with Jesus looks like. If you are a believer and you are anything like me, you might have immediately moved on to the next section after realizing I wasn't talking to you. But sometimes God exposes us to information that is not for us personally, but for someone else who He will put in our path. Whether you skipped it, skimmed it, or read it thoroughly, now may be a good time to go back to that section *(MAKE ROOM IN YOUR HEART,* particularly the *ABCs)* for reference.

Many of us who already know Jesus, still have a difficult time articulating what life in Him looks like. Specifically, we may struggle to explain how to enter into the relationship when talking to others who do not know Him. We have a sincere desire to tell people about Jesus, what He has done in our lives, and how to accept Him as Savior. But we often don't know where to start. The *ABC* explanation I shared earlier is just one of the many tools that can help us to have an answer when someone asks.

The best news is we are not alone. We must do our part to know God's Word and consider how we can share His truth. But we also have the Holy Spirit who helps us and teaches us and gives us words to speak.

In the next two chapters about putting others above ourselves, we will talk about spreading the love of Jesus through our actions.

# 12 Ways of Christmas

**PRAY:**
*Lord God, give me boldness to spread the word about the good news of Jesus. May others see who You are as I invite You into the celebration this Christmas. Bring to mind anyone who I can invite to church, and give me the courage to ask. Please give me opportunities to share Your love by inviting others into my story, and help me to communicate clearly about having a relationship with You. In Jesus' name, amen.*


**MEDITATE OR MEMORIZE:**
"When they had seen him, they spread the word concerning what had been told them about this child, and all who heard it were amazed at what the shepherds said to them." Luke 2:17-18

"The Word became flesh and made his dwelling among us. We have seen his glory, the glory of the one and only Son, who came from the Father, full of grace and truth." John 1:14

"Therefore go and make disciples of all nations, baptizing them in the name of the Father and of the Son and of the Holy Spirit, and teaching them to obey everything I have commanded you. And surely I am with you always, to the very end of the age." Matthew 28:19-20


**CONSIDER:**
1. Respond to the idea, "The Greatest Commandment is fulfilled in the Great Commission."

2. Write down the names of the people you want to invite to church this Christmas.

# Way 5- Others: Spread the Word

3. Start writing your story using the 3 questions: What was my life like before Jesus? How did I come to receive Him as my Savior? How has my life changed in relationship with Jesus?

4. Who would you like to invite into your story by telling them about your relationship with Jesus?

5. How would you articulate receiving salvation? Do you know another tool besides the *ABC* explanation?

# Way 6- You:

# Choose Joy

"At that time Mary got ready and hurried to a town in the hill country of Judea, where she entered Zechariah's home and greeted Elizabeth. When Elizabeth heard Mary's greeting, the baby leaped in her womb, and Elizabeth was filled with the Holy Spirit. In a loud voice she exclaimed: 'Blessed are you among women, and blessed is the child you will bear! But why am I so favored, that the mother of my Lord should come to me? As soon as the sound of your greeting reached my ears, the baby in my womb leaped for joy.'" Luke 1:39-44

An angel of the Lord had appeared to Mary and told her she would give birth to the Messiah. Mary hurried off to see her cousin Elizabeth who was pregnant with a miracle baby too, John the Baptist, the prophesied forerunner of Christ. While in his mother's womb, John leaped for joy being in the company of Jesus!

One chapter later in Luke's telling of the Savior's birth, an angel brings the shepherds "Good news that will cause great joy for all people." At Christmas, we celebrate Jesus who came to earth to be God with us. His presence is a cause for joy!

# 12 Ways of Christmas

**Fake Smiles**

*Elf* is one of the best Christmas movies ev-er, and Buddy the Elf is my kindred spirit. I love to smile! Smiling is my favorite! But when I'm not smiling, whether I'm concentrating or my face is at rest, people frequently ask me, "What's wrong?" And it's not just people who don't know me well that mistake my expressions. My very own family—the husband I have been married to for over two decades and the teenage boy I gave birth to—they often ask in a put-off tone, "Why are you making that face?" When I reply I'm not making any face at all, they push back harder. Clearly, the face means something.

Many years ago, I was struggling at work, at home, and with some mystery health issues which either caused or at least compounded all the other stresses. During a performance review at work, my boss talked to me about "making faces" in meetings. When I insisted I had no idea what he was talking about, he replied, "See, you're doing it right now." I promise, I did not intentionally make faces, but I couldn't see what apparently everyone else could.

My spirit was heavy from the whole weight of my life, and that conversation was a breaking point. I always strive for excellence in everything I do, so I would not let my work performance be affected by this issue, but I really didn't know how to fix it. I had heard the phrase, "Fake it 'til you make it," and thought, "I can do that." I sure wasn't feeling it, but I determined to plaster a big fake smile on my face. All. Day. Long. I sincerely tried, but my boss rolled his eyes at my silly expression in the morning meeting. By the end of the day, my face hurt and so did my heart. The fake smile on the outside did not heal or in the least bit cover up my brokenness on the inside.

Listen, pretending to be happy is not equivalent to choosing joy. Not even close. Choosing joy is not lived out by

# Way 6- You: Choose Joy

channeling Pollyanna, looking on the sunny side, and pretending we don't have a care in the world. A joyful life does not consist of putting on a happy face. However, when we lean in to embrace joy, we realize we have a reason to smile.

James 1:2-3 tells us to "Consider it pure joy, my brothers and sisters, whenever you face trials of many kinds, because you know the testing of your faith produces perseverance."

You see, joy is not a happy feeling based on our external circumstances. We can choose joy even in the middle of suffering knowing God is at work in our lives. This kind of joy is grown as we learn to love God with all our being. When we develop a deep conviction of His goodness and love towards us, we will believe His promises and trust Him with the outcome of our lives. That is a cause for joy!

Joy is awareness of God's grace, which is His unmerited favor in our lives. It's every blessing, every good and perfect gift. Choosing joy is letting God's grace change us on the inside. We are not subject to our feelings; we can feel feelings without indulging in them. Our circumstances may not change, but our hearts and minds and approach to life can change as we focus on the gift of God's unmerited grace. Joy supersedes what is happening around us; it is a choice. We can decide to respond with joy.

The world's pattern is to be tossed about by our circumstances and driven by our emotions. When our minds are renewed we can actively choose joy. It's a choice we have to make again and again.

**What does it look like to Choose Joy?**

Galatians 5:22-23 (NASB) states, "But the fruit of the Spirit is love, joy, peace, patience, kindness, goodness, faithfulness, gentleness and self-control; against such things there is no law." Joy is a fruit of the Spirit. It is the result of relationship with Jesus in which the Holy Spirit takes up residence in us. This means it is something we cannot manufacture for ourselves. To *Choose Joy* means to receive the joy that has been provided for us in Christ and to partner with the Holy Spirit in cultivating the fruit that only He produces. When we make the conditions right for joy to grow in our hearts, it will become our natural response.

Choosing joy is not like flipping a switch to turn us from Eeyore to Tigger. It is making one conscious decision at a time; to move forward and walk in step with the Spirit as He brings about fruit in our lives.

CHOOSE JOY IN YOUR HEART:
**Ask God.** As Christians, we sometimes get caught up in *supposed to*. Like, because the fruit of the Spirit includes joy, I'm *supposed to* have joy. Then, when we're not feeling so very joyful, instead of asking God for help, we become ashamed. Know this, not feeling joyful is not a reason for condemnation. In fact, joy is not based on our emotions at all.

God loves you; He sees you; He hears you. He wants you to have fullness of joy. If your joy is depleted, He invites you to ask Him to restore it. And remember how God gives? Generously and without finding fault. When you are not experiencing joy, God does not condemn you and ask you to work harder to obtain it. Instead, He welcomes you with open arms to join Him in cultivating joy.

The psalmist set an example for us, demonstrating how we might ask God for renewed joy.

"Restore to me the joy of your salvation and grant me a willing spirit, to sustain me." Psalm 51:12

Cultivating joy begins with asking God to produce the fruit of joy in our lives, to show us anything that is inhibiting our joy, and to enable us to make the conditions right for joy to grow.

# Way 6- You: Choose Joy

**\*Gratitude.** During November, I usually celebrate #gratitudemonth by posting daily "Give Thanks" prompts on social media. And it's always fun to go around the table before Thanksgiving dinner telling what we're thankful for. But, giving thanks should not end when the Black Friday shopping begins.

Gratitude is an act of choosing joy. There is a direct correlation between the amount of gratitude we express and the level of joy we experience. Gratitude shifts our focus from the things that cause stress to the only One who brings true rest. It places our attention on the good things in our lives and the Giver of every blessing.

I keep a gratitude list in the front of my prayer journal. And if you don't do it already, I want to encourage you to find your own way to keep track of the things you are thankful for—your praises, blessings, and answers to prayer. This practice solidifies the gratitude in our hearts as we write it down, and also gives us a record to remember the goodness and faithfulness of God.

Gratitude continues from documentation to expression. It's not enough to list what we're thankful for, gratitude extends to giving thanks to God for our blessings. And choosing joy takes gratitude one step further, bringing about an internal change that informs how we respond. The posture of our hearts becomes an attitude of gratitude.

**\*Rejoice.** Christmas should be a celebration not just a commemoration of our Savior's birth. When the wise men found Jesus, Matthew 2:10 (NASB) tells us they, "Rejoiced exceedingly with great joy." This holy day is not a somber religious occasion. That's why we wish others a Merry Christmas. The season is supposed to be fun, lively, and full of cheer. The festivities of Christmas bring with them expressions of joy. Laugh! Sing! Make merry! Rejoice!

Last Christmas, my friend Lil preached a message on joy, and I have carried this phrase with me. "It is a choice to

## 12 Ways of Christmas

rejoice!" To rejoice is an expression of joy, and it means to be glad for grace. We can choose joy by giving voice to our gladness.

"Rejoice always." 1Thessalonians 5:16
"Make a joyful noise to the LORD, all the earth." Psalm 100:1 (ESV)
"Rejoice in the Lord always. I will say it again: Rejoice!" Philippians 4:4
"This is the day that the Lord has made; let us rejoice and be glad in it." Psalm 118:24 (ESV)
"Sing, Daughter Zion; shout aloud, Israel! Be glad and rejoice with all your heart, Daughter Jerusalem!" Zephaniah 3:14

CHOOSE JOY IN YOUR ACTIVITIES:

In the busyness of the season, we must be intentional to enjoy—to actively take joy in—the wonder of Christmas. Joy and happiness are not synonymous. We know joy is a fruit of the Spirit; happiness is tied to our emotions and therefore our circumstances. While happiness is not joy, intentionally addressing the external factors that affect our happiness can facilitate our ability to cultivate joy.

One of the definitions for the Greek word translated *joy* in the New Testament is *delight*. When we approach the holiday season, let's engage in activities that bring delight (not dread).

Maybe you've heard of the home organization trend instructing us to get rid of any possessions that do not "spark joy." When I look in my closet, almost everything I own is either worn out, stretched out, or too small. That does not spark joy. If I only kept what sparked joy, I'd be left with my winter coat and one pair of cozy socks. Some things, like covering our bodies with clothes, are necessary for functionality.

In the same way, as we sort delightful versus dreadful activities, we may have to keep some things that do not spark

# Way 6- You: Choose Joy

joy but are necessary for doing life. The encouragement to select activities that bring delight comes with the caveat that we likely have responsibilities we do not enjoy but are part of being a grown adult.

So what does it mean to do what brings delight (not dread)? Joy is a choice, and there are hundreds of choices we make every day that either contribute to our joy or steal it.

**\*Relationships.** Many gatherings take place during the holidays. Whether it's work, school, church, community, or family, these gatherings have one thing in common. People. And people are messy. Sometimes obligations or traditions mean our schedules include activities and interactions we do not prefer. But when it is within our ability to decide, we need to spend our time in ways that cultivate joy. This means limiting our exposure to people who drain us and intentionally connecting with those who fill our cups. As I looked back to evaluate "Our First Best Christmas," I realized our schedule reflected this principle seemingly by chance, but the result was an obvious increase in enjoyment.

Sometimes there are people who we like, even love, and we sincerely want to spend time with them. But we can only tolerate those people in increments. You probably have someone like that in your life. You know how after you've been together, you feel like you need a nap? Pay attention to how much time you're able to spend with someone before it gets to be too much, and end the interaction before you get to that point. You are not obligated to engage past your limit or let people overstay their welcome.

Inform Aunt Betty you will be leaving her house after two hours. Invite your guests to come for dinner from 5:00 to 8:00. Tell your in-laws they are welcome to stay for one night. I mean, don't be rude and say, "After that, you start to get on my nerves." You don't even need to give a reason. "I have to go (or you have to go) at that time," is a good enough response. It is not only okay; it is actually healthy for your relationships to set boundaries that guard your joy. If the other person refuses to respect your boundaries, you may need to spend even less time with them.

Needing to limit your time with others does not always mean there is something wrong with them or with you, for that matter. Western culture has made us protective of our personal space. If you are an introvert who recharges by spending time alone, this is especially true for you. I'm an extreme extrovert. I love all the people all day long! This is what energizes me! But at the end of the day, I need to go home to my own space where there is no need to be "on."

I have a handful of friends who being with them is like plugging in. Even if I'm exhausted, I'm somehow invigorated by their presence. And I need that most during the holiday season when I am constantly feeling depleted. With these friends, we never part ways because we are bored or there's nothing left to talk about. It's always unfortunate when it's time to go. I hope you have people like this in your life. If you do, don't let Christmas go by without connecting. Chances are you fill them up too.

If you don't have people like this, it might have stung a little bit when you read the last paragraph. I hope you can hear my heart. We know we're better together. But sometimes we keep putting ourselves out there, and we can't figure out why we haven't found "our people" yet. That was true for me. When I scrolled through and saw what seemed like everybody else posting Instagram BFF selfies, I threw my phone down and shouted with a tear burning down my cheek, "What's wrong with me? What do I have to do to have that?" The answer is, I don't know. I'm sorry. I don't know why some of us don't have fulfilling friendships, and I don't know why it took so long for me to find them. But I do know the desire in our hearts for this connection is from God. He made us for community, and He wants to fulfill that longing in us. Oh, I wish we had more time together to talk about this. But I just

# Way 6- You: Choose Joy

want to encourage you not to give up on seeking meaningful relationships. Keep showing up. Keep asking God. Keep trusting Him.

While this chapter is about caring for ourselves, God is often so gracious to fulfill our needs as we meet the needs of others. Be the friend you want to have and fill somebody else's cup. We can choose joy by spreading joy!

***Feasts.** Some of the holy days described in the Old Testament call for feasting and others (like the Day of Atonement) command fasting. Christmas is not prescribed as one of those holy days, so we don't have an outline for how God expects us to celebrate. Food is my love language, and I spend an inordinate amount of time talking and dreaming about what may be on "The Lord's Banquet Table." So, it would be no surprise that I would lean towards Christmas being a feasting holiday and save the fasting for Lent.

I do not know your specific situation, so please view my personal commentary in light of your own lifestyle, dietary needs, and health concerns. I have spent a few holiday seasons "dieting" and miserable. It did not cultivate joy for me when I was chomping on a dry baby carrot while watching as my family members savored the traditional Santa Claus cookies we looked forward to every Christmas. On the other hand, in those years when I binged on holiday goodies with no regard, I was left feeling guilty and bloated in January.

Over and over, moderation is encouraged throughout the Bible, because it truly is the way we ought to live. All of the *You* sections in this book are focused on caring for ourselves in a balanced way. I think this is a good place to remember balance. We can enjoy without overindulging. Eating one Christmas cut-out after I have been attentive to my food choices the rest of the day is delightful. Mindlessly eating the entire tray of Christmas cookies plus fudge and buckeyes only feels good until the sugar buzz wears off. Dread sets in when my pants don't fit in the New Year. December might not be

## 12 Ways of Christmas

the best time to start a super restrictive eating plan. However, it's never a bad time to begin making one good choice after another. So my suggestion is that we do not deprive ourselves during the holidays and miss out, but that we are also not gluttonous so we regret it in the time to come. We can both enjoy the moment and be mindful of the future

*Tasks. When it is within our power to decide, we should minimize activities that deplete us and make time for activities that energize us. If it makes you happy to shop 'til you drop and perfectly wrap dozens of packages, adorning each with a handmade bow, do it with gusto! But if there's a pit in your stomach thinking about crowds and paper and folding and taping, then, by all means, improvise. Shop online. Place presents in gift bags. Pay someone else to wrap. Or just buy gift cards. We could imagine similar scenarios for every holiday endeavor, but you will certainly come up with your own ideas specific to your celebrations.

Here's where you could create another list. Make 2 columns. Write on one side what brings you delight at the holidays and on the other side what you dread. Pray about and brainstorm ways to engage in the "delight" column and ways to avoid or better deal with the "dread" column. Whatever you do, don't make yourself miserable by thinking you have to do all the things and be all the things.

I get all starry-eyed dreaming of drive-thru light shows and holiday concerts and snuggling on the couch watching all the Christmas classics. There might be a little twinkle in your eye when you think about undertaking one or two items on the "delight" side of your own list. Give yourself permission to do it. In fact, boss yourself around a bit and insist that you take time for what you enjoy at Christmas.

At some point, we do have to put on our big girl pants and address unavoidable, or maybe even dreadful tasks. As we approach those things, remember back to the words in James

# Way 6- You: Choose Joy

1:2-3. Let's look for opportunities to "consider it pure joy" in every situation by keeping in mind the result.

Guess what? Doing dishes and laundry does not bring me delight. Does that mean I should make my family wear dirty clothes and only eat take-out for the entire month of December? It's tempting, but I suppose not.

Washing dishes does not bring me joy but having a clean kitchen does.

Folding laundry is not delightful but fresh, clean, wrinkle-free clothing is.

You get the point. Life isn't all fun, but fulfilling our purpose is satisfying. We can choose joy even in the dreadful and mundane when we consider the good produced.

Even when we carefully select our undertakings, the activity of the holidays can leave us depleted. In Nehemiah 8:10 we see "the joy of the Lord is our strength." Choosing joy at Christmas means daily receiving God's strength so we don't just survive but thrive during the season.

**PRAY:**
*Oh God, thank You for the Holy Spirit who produces the fruit of joy in my life. Please show me anything that inhibits my joy and teach me to partner with You in cultivating joy during the holiday season. In every situation, may I be glad for Your grace and intentional to choose joy. In Jesus' name, amen.*

**MEDITATE OR MEMORIZE:**
"Consider it pure joy, my brothers and sisters, whenever you face trials of many kinds, because you know the testing of your faith produces perseverance." James 1:2-3

"But the fruit of the Spirit is love, joy, peace, patience, kindness, goodness, faithfulness, gentleness and self-control;

## 12 Ways of Christmas

against such things there is no law." Galatians 5:22-23 (NASB)

"Restore to me the joy of your salvation and grant me a willing spirit, to sustain me." Psalm 51:12

**CONSIDER:**
1. How is it possible to choose joy in the midst of trials?

2. What would it look like for you to partner with the Holy Spirit to cultivate joy?

3. How does gratitude affect your joy?

4. Who fills your cup? How will you intentionally connect with them at Christmas?

5. What are some ways to do what brings delight (not dread)?

# Way 7- Jesus:

# Worship Him

"And Mary said:
'My soul glorifies the Lord and my spirit rejoices in God my Savior, for he has been mindful of the humble state of his servant. From now on all generations will call me blessed, for the Mighty One has done great things for me—holy is his name. His mercy extends to those who fear him, from generation to generation. He has performed mighty deeds with his arm; he has scattered those who are proud in their inmost thoughts. He has brought down rulers from their thrones but has lifted up the humble. He has filled the hungry with good things but has sent the rich away empty. He has helped his servant Israel, remembering to be merciful to Abraham and his descendants forever, just as he promised our ancestors.'"
Luke 1:46-55

In the last chapter, we left off in Scripture at the part of the Christmas story where Mary visited her cousin Elizabeth. What comes next is the passage above, often referred to as "Mary's Song" (or "The Magnificat" if you prefer the Latin term.) In this intimate moment between Mary and her God, we see a beautiful expression and example of worship.

# 12 Ways of Christmas

### Christmas Music

Grandma Phyllis had a beautiful piece of maple furniture that stretched along nearly the entire wall in her living room. Most of the time, it served as a display table for décor. But on Christmas Eve, Grandma removed her mother's handmade doily and the porcelain vase of dried wildflowers that we had gathered in the fall. Once a year, when she lifted the lid, that ordinary sidebar was transformed into a merry-making machine. She opened the cupboard beneath, carefully removed a classic Christmas vinyl from its yellowed paper jacket, and placed it on the turntable. Even today, Christmas music instantly puts a little pep in my step as it transports me back to those childhood memories.

Look, Christmas music is just happy! Even a melancholy song like *I'll be Home for Christmas* is heartwarming. But to be honest, it's a surface-level feeling that doesn't last long. I'm all about doing a little *Jingle Bell Rock,* so, understand that I would never condemn getting your cheer on with a holiday playlist. In fact, as we talked about in *Choose Joy*, I believe celebrating the season with entertainment adds to our delight. Still, I need more than a temporary mood lift in an attempt to conjure up the Christmas spirit. I require a heart shift to cultivate a restful holiday season.

On "Our First Best Christmas" I discovered the impact of worship almost accidentally. I had secured tickets for myself and five of the ladies from my Tuesday night small group to attend a Christmas concert featuring *For King and Country*. Purchasing the tickets entered me into a drawing to win a signed copy of their latest Christmas CD. And guess what? I won!

I had forgotten about it until the day a package arrived in the mail. After struggling for 10 minutes to free the disc from the cellophane wrapper, I popped it into the player. My son listened with me, and we were blown away by the very first song *Little Drummer Boy*. That song has always been a

# Way 7- Jesus: Worship Him

favorite for our family, but if you haven't heard this version, girl, finish this chapter, then go search it. Asa and I enjoyed the music so much, we incorporated it into the start of our day for the entire month of December.

At first, I just listened, soaking in the melodies and lyrics (and the percussion!), filling my heart and mind with words about Jesus. Half of the songs were familiar classics, and the others became nearly instant favorites. Soon, I began to sing along. Something shifted as I said the words out loud engaging my senses, and my faith was bolstered as I sang truths about our Lord. This was more than the enhanced mood I got from jamming to classic holiday tunes. This Christ-centered Christmas music was feeding my soul.

Worship directly contributes to alleviating the stress of the holiday season. But while reduced stress is often the result, it is not the reason why we worship. You see, I don't worship as a remedy for my anxious thoughts. When I feel anxious it is an indicator that my mind is focused on my circumstances rather than on my Savior.

Remember, this chapter isn't about us; our focus at this moment is loving God with all of our being through worshiping Him. Worship is more than the music itself, more than singing along, and even more than what we get out of it. When I was a kid, I thought worship was the time during the song service on Sunday morning when we sang slow songs and lifted our hands. That is, as opposed to praise, which was when we clapped in rhythm with the fast songs. Singing can be a vehicle for our worship, but it is not the definition. True worship is a posture of turning our hearts to God. As I sang along to the music, the full impact of worship took hold in those moments when I shifted from singing *about* God and began singing *to* Him.

When we worship Him, fix our eyes on Jesus, and put Him in His rightful place at the center of our lives, our hearts are set right. Worship is for God, not for us, but in His goodness,

# 12 Ways of Christmas

God often allows our souls to be blessed as we bring Him praise.

### What does it look like to Worship Him?

To *Worship Him* means to turn our hearts to God in an expression of reverence and adoration. The word *worship* is essentially *worth*-ship, proclaiming the greatness of God.

My church sets aside time for worship during the service every Sunday; yours probably does too. I cry during that time of corporate worship. Nearly. Every. Time. I'm not sad. I'm overcome—by the goodness of God, and by communion with my brothers and sisters in Christ as we lift praise to His name in unity. My emotional response is not the purpose of worship. I say this because I used to be confused about that, and I thought maybe I'm not the only one. I once believed that worship was about a feeling. Kind of like the nostalgic experience of listening to Christmas music; I thought worship was about the experience.

The leaders in our churches serve us by creating an environment conducive to worship. They limit external distractions and lead us in songs that glorify God. Oh, I hope we take full advantage of that dedicated time by limiting internal distractions and truly turning our hearts to our Father. But we need to remember, worship is not confined to the church building during service time. I have engaged authentic worship at my kitchen sink with my hands dunked in dishwater as equally as in the sanctuary with my hands lifted in the air. Worship is not about our physical location or the position of our bodies but the posture of our hearts.

Jesus addressed this in a conversation with a Samaritan woman at Jacob's Well. In the middle of their conversation, the woman questioned the proper location for worship.

"'Sir,' the woman said, 'I can see that you are a prophet. Our ancestors worshiped on this mountain, but you Jews claim

# Way 7- Jesus: Worship Him

that the place where we must worship is in Jerusalem.' 'Woman,' Jesus replied, 'believe me, a time is coming when you will worship the Father neither on this mountain nor in Jerusalem. You Samaritans worship what you do not know; we worship what we do know, for salvation is from the Jews. Yet a time is coming and has now come when the true worshipers will worship the Father in the Spirit and in truth, for they are the kind of worshipers the Father seeks. God is spirit, and his worshipers must worship in the Spirit and in truth." John 4:19-24

Jesus broke down the barriers for all believers when He explained true worship. It isn't ceremony or ritual dependent on where we are and what we are doing.

Hebrews 12:28 gives us a glimpse of what true worship looks like. "Therefore, since we are receiving a kingdom that cannot be shaken, let us be thankful, and so worship God acceptably with reverence and awe." You see, worship is determined by the posture of our hearts, and often our bodies follow in an expression of humility and respect. In fact, the word that Jesus used in the verse above translated *worship* has the literal meaning of *kneeling in reverence.*

True worship is about genuine connection, authentic communion with God. He is most concerned with the proximity of our spirits to His. God desires our worship and is seeking out those who will worship Him with sincerity.

We see several examples of true worship in the Bible narrative of the Christmas story. The characters worshiped God for who He is, for what He has done, and for what He promised to do.

WORSHIP HIM FOR WHO HE IS:

In *Seek Him,* we encountered the Magi. Remember, the purpose of their pilgrimage and ours—of seeking Him and finding Him—is to worship. Matthew 2:11 tells us, "On coming to the house, they saw the child with his mother Mary, and they bowed down and worshiped Him." The Magi worshiped Jesus for Who He is. They recognized Him to be "the king of the Jews," the fulfillment of prophecy.

One simple way we can worship God is to focus on His names and attributes that we find in the Bible. Here are some examples of what Scripture says about who He is:

**\*Names of God:**
"Come, let us bow down in worship, let us kneel before **the LORD our Maker**." Psalm 95:6

"For to us a child is born, to us a son is given, and the government will be on his shoulders. And he will be called **Wonderful Counselor, Mighty God, Everlasting Father, Prince of Peace**." Isaiah 9:6

"The Spirit you received does not make you slaves, so that you live in fear again; rather, the Spirit you received brought about your adoption to sonship. And by him we cry, '**Abba, Father**.'" Romans 8:15

"On his robe and on his thigh he has this name written: **king of kings** and **lord of lords**." Revelation 19:16

**\*Attributes of God:**
"The LORD, the LORD, the **compassionate** and **gracious** God, **slow to anger, abounding in love and faithfulness**." Exodus 34:6

"For the LORD is **good** and his love endures forever; his faithfulness continues through all generations." Psalm 100:5

"Let us hold unswervingly to the hope we profess, for he who promised is **faithful**." Hebrews 10:23

# Way 7- Jesus: Worship Him

"**Holy, holy, holy** is the Lord God **Almighty**,' who was, and is, and is to come." Revelation 4:8b

Many worship songs come straight from Scripture, and some of them may have come to mind as you read through these verses. Since we've had this conversation, it may hit us a little differently when we hear and sing the titles of God. I want to encourage you to search the Scripture for yourself to find more names and attributes you can employ to worship God for who He is. Thank God for being these things to you as you turn your heart to Him in worship.

WORSHIP HIM FOR WHAT HE HAS DONE:
In Luke 2:20, we see that after the shepherds' encounter with Jesus, they "returned, glorifying and praising God for all the things they had heard and seen, which were just as they had been told." The shepherds worshiped God for what He had done. He revealed Himself to them and pointed them to Jesus.

What has God done for you? What have you heard and seen that is a cause for worship? If you have been documenting gratitude like we talked about in the last chapter, you can incorporate the things you are thankful for into your worship. Worshiping God for what He has done can also include examples of God's faithfulness in His Word.

"In the beginning God **created the heavens and the earth**." Genesis 1:1

"So God **created mankind in his own image**, in the image of God he created them; male and female he created them." Genesis 1:27

"He **provided redemption for his people**; he **ordained his covenant forever**-- holy and awesome is his name." Psalm 111:9

"The next day John saw Jesus coming toward him and said, 'Look, the Lamb of God, who **takes away the sin of the world!**'" John 1:29

"But God **demonstrates his own love for us** in this: While we were still sinners, Christ **died for us**." Romans 5:8

Remember all that God has done for you as you worship Him.

WORSHIP HIM FOR WHAT HE PROMISES TO DO:
In our opening passage, we saw that, like the wise men, Mary worshiped God for who He is when she called Him, "God my Savior," "Mighty One," and said, "Holy is his name."

In the same way as the shepherds, Mary worshiped God for what He had done. "He has been mindful of the humble state of his servant," "He has done great things for me," and "He has performed mighty deeds with his arm."

There's one verse we haven't looked at yet, between the part of the Christmas story where John the Baptist leaped for joy in Elizabeth's womb and the part where we read Mary's song. In Luke 1:45 Elizabeth said of Mary, "Blessed is she who believed that the Lord would fulfill His promise to her!"

Mary believed God. The baby Jesus was growing in her womb but had not yet fulfilled the promise to save His people. Mary did not wait until Jesus was born or until he began His public ministry thirty years later. She worshiped God for the promise He had given before she ever saw the result. "He has helped his servant Israel, remembering to be merciful to Abraham and his descendants forever, just as he promised our ancestors." Mary worshiped God for what He promised to do.

I know we've heard people say, "I'll believe it when I see it." That wasn't Mary's attitude. We can follow her example, and worship God for His promises before we see them fulfilled.

## Way 7- Jesus: Worship Him

Maybe sometimes the promises in Scripture are difficult for us to believe when things don't seem to be going our way. And it is definitely easier to encourage our friends with God's promises and believe He will act on their behalf. Sister, if you've met me, online or in person, you've probably heard me say this before, and I will never get tired of repeating it. (In fact, I'm going to type it in all caps because this truth gets me so excited, I can't help but shout it!) GOD'S PROMISES ARE TRUE, AND THEY ARE FOR YOU!

Our Father is a Promise Maker and Promise Keeper. When we consider His promises, we can worship God in advance, even when we don't see it or feel it, because we know that He is faithful to His Word. Let's look at a few promises from Scripture that we can use to worship Him.

"**The LORD will fight for you**; you need only to be still." Exodus 14:14

"And we know that **in all things God works for the good of those who love him**, who have been called according to his purpose." Romans 8:28

"Being confident of this, that **he who began a good work in you will carry it on to completion** until the day of Christ Jesus." Philippians 1:6

"And **my God will meet all your needs** according to the riches of his glory in Christ Jesus." Philippians 4:19

"God has said, '**Never will I leave you; never will I forsake you.**'" Hebrews 13:5b

Trust God to keep His promises as you worship Him for what He will do.

# 12 Ways of Christmas

WORSHIP HIM WITH YOUR LIFE:
"Therefore, I urge you, brothers and sisters, in view of God's mercy, to offer your bodies as a living sacrifice, holy and pleasing to God—this is your true and proper worship." Romans 12:1

The word *worship* here is not the same word we saw the Magi and Jesus use earlier. This word translated *worship* in Romans carries the meaning of *service rendered to God in worship*. It goes beyond the expression and connection to God in worship and informs the way we live a life of worship through service.

Offering ourselves as a sacrifice to God is willingly giving Him control. Spiritual surrender is not a matter of throwing up the white flag and giving up. It is not saying with slumped shoulders and a woeful expression, "Fine, we'll do it your way, I guess." True worship with our lives includes laying down our selfish desires, but it also means picking up His will for our lives and adopting it as our own. It is a commitment to follow His plan because we trust Him. In this way, every aspect of our lives—work and play, the mundane and the extraordinary—can be offered up to Him as an act of worship. The ultimate expression of true worship is yielding our lives to be used by God for His purpose.

The world's pattern is for Christmas to be focused on our own experience; when our minds are renewed, we do everything for the glory of God.

## PRAY:

*Dear Lord, I desire to be a true worshiper, to worship You in spirit and in truth. May I worship You for who You are, what You have done, and what You promise to do. Teach me to continually turn my heart to You, making my whole life an expression of worship. In Jesus' name, amen.*

# Way 7- Jesus: Worship Him

**MEDITATE OR MEMORIZE:**
"And Mary said: 'My soul glorifies the Lord and my spirit rejoices in God my Savior.'" Luke 1:46-47

"God is spirit, and his worshipers must worship in the Spirit and in truth." John 4:24

"Therefore, I urge you, brothers and sisters, in view of God's mercy, to offer your bodies as a living sacrifice, holy and pleasing to God--this is your true and proper worship." Romans 12:1

**CONSIDER:**
1. In your own words, describe true worship.

2. List some names and attributes of God. Why are those titles meaningful to you?

3. What comes to mind as you consider what God has done?

4. Which promises of God are you standing on and worshiping Him for?

5. In what way could you offer up every aspect of your life as an act of worship?

# Way 8- Others:

# Give Intentionally

"For God so loved the world that he gave his one and only Son, that whoever believes in him shall not perish but have eternal life." John 3:16

"This is how we know what love is: Jesus Christ laid down his life for us. And we ought to lay down our lives for our brothers and sisters." 1 John 3:16

(Jesus said) "No one takes it from me, but I lay it down of my own accord. I have authority to lay it down and authority to take it up again. This command I received from my Father." John 10:18

At Christmas, we celebrate the greatest gift—Jesus. God gave the gift of His only Son because of His love for each and every person. The Father did this knowing the full extent of His plan—that the manger would lead to the cross. And Jesus was not an unwilling participant. The apostle John tells us in his Gospel and in his first epistle, that Jesus laid Himself down. Thirty-three years after taking on human form and arriving in Bethlehem, Jesus willingly gave up His life so we could have the gift of eternal life.

The true meaning of Christmas is that Jesus came from Heaven to earth to pave the way for humanity's restored relationship to God. He is Immanuel, God with us. I've heard

## 12 Ways of Christmas

it said this way, "Christmas is not about the presents, but the Presence." We do not want to conform to the world's materialistic view that morphs Christmas into nothing more than a gift-giving occasion. However, giving in the right spirit at the holidays can be a beautiful expression of our gratitude for all God has given us. When we give intentionally it is an outpouring of His love and our own love for others.

**The Perfect Gift**

My quest for the perfect gift began in the second grade. A few days before the holiday break, each class took turns visiting the "Santa Shop" in the school cafeteria where lunch tables were covered in all sorts of crafty items and novelties. In preparation for my very first solo shopping trip, I tucked $2 into my sweater before getting on the bus that morning.

I squirmed in my seat all day until it was finally time for Mrs. Kline's class to shop. On the third table was a treat I could not pass up. Candy airplanes—a roll of Life Savers made up the body of the plane, two individual Life Savers formed the landing gear, and a stick of Wrigley's chewing gum completed the aircraft representing the wings on top. I bought four, one for each of my brothers and one for myself.

With a dollar left burning a hole in my pocket, I scanned the room looking for the next purchase. My eyes landed on just the thing. An embroidered leather cowboy boot key chain. My friend Andrew wore cowboy boots to church every week. It would be the perfect present for him, and I chose the nicest one. Hours and days passed slowly until the next Sunday when I could give my friend his gift. Andrew ripped the edges of the wrapping paper scrap I had gotten from my mom. I waited to see excitement on his face that never came. Andrew held the boot in his hand with a puzzled look. He glanced up at me and said "White cowboy boots are for girls. You can keep it if you want." I'm not gonna lie; I was actually a little

## Way 8- Others: Give Intentionally

excited to have the keychain for myself. Still, I was disappointed that my gift wasn't good enough. I honestly thought the pristine white cowboy boot looked so much nicer than those dull brown and black boots, and I hoped my friend would think so too.

The search for the elusive perfect gift went on for decades. Until one Christmas when I finally nailed it. It had become a Thanksgiving tradition that after the dinner table was cleared and wiped clean, Black Friday ads were spread out to thumb through. I squealed with delight when I came across a video-gaming chair with built-in speakers. There was no doubt my Xbox-crazed middle nephew would love it, and while normally it would have been way out of my price range, this special sale put the chair right within my budget.

Christmas Eve did not disappoint. That kid opened his package with a fist pump and shouted "Yes!" Then he immediately ran across the room to hug me. A couple of weeks later, when the tree had been lugged back down to the basement and the Christmas buzz had worn off, my nephew walked into my kitchen and handed me a certificate. "Aunt of the Year Award." I knew he would like the present and that he was always grateful, but I never expected him to make such a gesture.

You would think that having won Christmas that year would have completed my mission. But hitting the mark that one time for that one person didn't bring the satisfaction I had hoped. The certificate hung on my refrigerator as a reminder, and the pursuit only intensified as I set out to continue earning that award year after year.

Giving good gifts at Christmas can be both a joy and a stressor. My endless search led to exhaustion and disappointment for many years until I realized it is impossible to get the perfect gift for every person every time. Instead, I

# 12 Ways of Christmas

shifted my focus to giving intentional gifts, and that led to a more restful holiday season.

### What does it look like to Give Intentionally to Others?

The definition of the word *intentional* is to do on purpose. I love that! To *Give Intentionally* means to give with purpose, to pay careful consideration to what we will give and who will receive. Impulsive giving is consistent with the world's way of doing Christmas. Intentional giving is the result of a renewed mind.

PURPOSE TO GIVE:
**\*Give with the right motivation.** "So when you give to the needy, do not announce it with trumpets, as the hypocrites do in the synagogues and on the streets, to be honored by others. Truly I tell you, they have received their reward in full." Matthew 6:2

The verse above was specifically referring to the Pharisees who would make a big show of their giving to the poor in order to draw attention to themselves. Whether we are talking about charitable giving or giving presents, this Scripture is a warning to check our hearts. We can determine our motivation by examining the purpose of our giving. Let's think about why we give gifts at Christmas.

There are all kinds of reasons why we give. Tradition. Obligation. Expectation.

One thing that always squashed my gift-giving good vibes was expectation. Of course, there was my own expectation of finding the perfect gift. To tell the truth, sometimes I was more excited about the present itself than the person I gave to. But I also held some expectations of the receiver of the gift. I looked for what I deemed to be an appropriate response and often anticipated receiving in return. To cultivate a restful Christmas, we must let go of expectations.

# Way 8- Others: Give Intentionally

When I consider my motivation in searching for the perfect gift, part of it was definitely to make the other person happy. But honestly, I was also in search of gratitude and affirmation and that good feeling I get from giving. Even now, I prefer for the other person to open their gift in front of me. That's okay because giving is relational, and we enjoy those shared moments. We just have to be careful that our purpose in giving isn't self-focused. Gratitude and good feelings may be side-effects of giving but they should not be the reason why we give.

When God gave His only Son and Jesus gave His life, the motivation was love. God loved the world so much that He gave His Son, and we know what love is because Jesus gave Himself.

When we focus on God's love for us and others, we can give with the same motivation. According to 1 John 4:19, "We love because He first loved us." So when we give intentionally, our motivation is both demonstrating God's love for others and loving others well with the love He has given us. Giving that is rooted in love is not self-seeking, it is thoughtful and generous.

**\*Give thoughtfully.** We know the perfect gift is an impossible aim that leads to disappointment. But when we give up on the notion of perfection, it can be easy to swing to the opposite side of the pendulum and give carelessly. It is possible to give considerate gifts that will be appreciated by the receiver without obsessing over the ideal.

Sometimes we make giving about us. We give the other person a present we would like to have for ourselves or something we want for them to have. As I get older, I realize how easy it is to get nostalgic at Christmas. I have to be careful not to fill my cart with my own favorite childhood toys or those I wish I had, without first considering whether the child who receives the gift would actually enjoy it.

# 12 Ways of Christmas

Being intentional to give thoughtful gifts is about leaning into relationship. If we want to give thoughtfully, we need to know the person we will be gifting. Throughout the year as we spend time with people, we should pay attention to things they like and enjoy.

If you haven't figured it out yet, I love lists. I have a list app on my phone and besides my grocery list and to-do list, there is a list for each of my closest people. I want to give thoughtfully, but my memory fails me when it's shopping time. So, throughout the year, I make little notes of things one of the grandkids pointed out in the store, or a friend posted about on social media, or my son mentioned in conversation. I also keep a private Christmas shopping list in my Amazon account so when I come across potential gift ideas, I save them there until I'm ready to make purchases.

Thoughtful giving will look different with an acquaintance than with a close friend or family member, but we can always pay attention and consider the receiver in order to give good gifts. The best way to be sure we give thoughtfully is to remember the purpose is an expression of love.

**\*Give generously.** "Command them to do good, to be rich in good deeds, and to be generous and willing to share." 1 Timothy 6:18

I don't know about you, but when we start talking about generosity, my mind immediately goes to extravagant gifts and grand gestures. You know, those commercials that air at Christmastime? A couple in matching pajamas walks out the front door of their home, the man's hand covering the woman's eyes. He slips his fingers away to reveal her surprise gift topped with a giant red bow. Cue the game show host voice, "It's a brand-new car!" In all my search for the perfect gift, I could never set the bar that high. And if you can't either, that doesn't mean we're falling short.

Being generous doesn't require giving over-the-top, expensive gifts. It is defined by the condition of the heart,

# Way 8- Others: Give Intentionally

being ready and willing to give. You see, generosity is not an amount; it's an attitude.

In Matthew chapter 10 when Jesus sent His disciples on their first mission, He said, "Freely you have received; freely give." In this context, Jesus was talking about the spreading of the gospel and the signs He had given them to accompany their message. The disciples were instructed to open-handedly give what they had received from God. And this concept applies to giving in every aspect of our lives. Generosity is a mindset that recognizes all that we have is a gift from God, and it compels us to share those gifts with others.

The example God set in giving the gift of Jesus was sacrificial. A sacrifice means we are giving something up. So a challenge for us during the holiday season is not that we would give beyond our means by going into debt, but to give more generously by foregoing some indulgence. Ask God to give you discernment about what you could sacrifice to give more generously this Christmas.

PLAN TO GIVE:
Giving intentionally means we must be prepared to give. Waiting until the last minute, going to the store with no ideas and no plan is stressful. It sets us up for impulsive buying and over-spending. Friends, celebrating the birth of our Savior in December should not leave us with a mountain of debt in the New Year. A financial burden can be a major contributor to the after-Christmas let-down that robs us of rest.

*Budget. Now, talking about budgeting may seem a little contradictory since we just wrapped up a conversation about generosity, but I assure you, it is not. Giving generously and giving within our means are not in opposition. Setting and sticking to a budget does not mean giving selfishly or sparingly, it is simply being a good steward of what God has entrusted to us. Managing our finances well includes both

## 12 Ways of Christmas

giving liberally and sensibly. In fact, in planning well, we will discover ways to give even more generously.

One of the distorted messages from the world's version of Christmas pushes us to top last year, go bigger and better, get more, spend more. But we don't have to follow the pattern of the world. Being transformed by God's Word gives us permission to honor Him by making prudent decisions about our holiday spending.

Second Corinthians 9:7 talks about intentional giving. "Each of you should give what you have decided in your heart to give, not reluctantly or under compulsion, for God loves a cheerful giver."

Oh, compulsion! That's my biggest Christmas budget downfall. I plan ahead and shop early at Christmas so I can give good, thoughtful gifts. This also keeps me from being stressed out by scrambling at the last minute. But in that space between when I have finished shopping and when our Christmas gatherings take place, I feel an urge to keep buying, keep spending, keep adding to the endless pile under the Christmas tree.

Last year, my gift list was complete, and I had spent my budget. But then, I was shopping for bath towels at TJ Maxx when I came across a super cute *Central Perk* coffee mug. Since our fourth granddaughter loves coffee and all things *Friends*, I simply had to buy it for her. It wasn't a big deal; it was only 5 bucks. But since I make every effort to give the kids an equal number of gifts and spend close to the same amount, that one small gift meant I needed to buy 5 more mugs. So $5 turned to $30. Unfortunately, it often keeps going and keeps escalating.

Honoring God with our gifts means we have to decide in our hearts what we will give, and we must not give compulsively. This approach of planning ahead and giving intentionally allows us to give cheerfully because we do not fear the credit card bills that will come in January.

# Way 8- Others: Give Intentionally

Our own expectations can cause stress during the holidays, but we aren't the only ones with expectations that need to be addressed. Sometimes we project our feelings onto other people and make assumptions about what they anticipate. But other times, our friends and family actually do hold us to a certain standard of giving.

So many years I relented. When I was asked to pitch in for a shared gift, and my portion was twice as much as I had planned to spend, I paid it rather than speak up. When a more distant relative bought an unexpected present, I felt obligated to buy a gift to match. I often purchased more than I was able because I figured it was expected. But on "Our First Best Christmas," I decided I wouldn't do it anymore. Taking a stand meant having some awkward conversations, but being a good steward was worth it. And the exchanges, while uncomfortable, were not as bad as I had built them up to be. I simply said, "We aren't buying for adults this year," and "We will be spending $25 for nieces and nephews." My family agreed or at least understood, and it was a relief not to go against my better judgment by overspending.

**\*Save and buy ahead.** Some people prepare for Christmas by saving money each month so they have a big chunk to spend in December. I buy most of my gifts after Thanksgiving, but I also plan ahead by picking up items throughout the year and stashing them away for the holidays.

Being frugal does not have to equal being stingy. In fact, I am often able to give more generous gifts by stretching my budget. As I go about my routine shopping, I stop by clearance racks and special sales. I know it's not what Jesus meant when He said "As you seek so shall you find." But the secret to finding good deals is looking for them.

I keep track of every purchase, both the amount I paid and the retail value. It's a challenge to give the best possible gift at the lowest possible price, and it's turned into a bit of a game for me. I do enjoy bragging rights when I tell my husband how much money I saved. But more so, it is a joy to be able to give twice, three times, and sometimes four times as much while sticking to my financial plan because I took the time to shop carefully.

***Give Charitably.** Most of our conversation about giving has been centered around the gifts purchased for our friends and family. The Bible reminds us to give to those who cannot give to us in return, and there are endless ways to do that during the holidays. As we plan to give at Christmas, let's keep in mind giving to those in need, as well as the missions and ministries that support them. Pray in advance about how God would lead you to give charitably. Include the amount in your budget, and be prepared to give.

Giving intentionally by planning ahead allows us to give more thoughtfully and more generously. It reduces the stress of shopping during the holidays and doesn't leave us financially strained. Most of all, it honors God when we are good stewards of what He has entrusted to us.

**PRAY:**
*Father, thank You for the gift of Your Son. Teach me to follow Your example, to give with purpose, rooted in love. Help me to give thoughtful gifts by leaning into relationship. May I be a good steward of all You have given. As I set a budget for Christmas giving, please give me the restraint to not give compulsively but within my means. Show me what sacrifices I can make to give more generously and may every gift honor You. In Jesus' name, amen.*

# Way 8- Others: Give Intentionally

**MEDITATE OR MEMORIZE:**
"For God so loved the world that he gave his one and only Son, that whoever believes in him shall not perish but have eternal life." John 3:16

"Command them to do good, to be rich in good deeds, and to be generous and willing to share." 1 Timothy 6:18

"Each of you should give what you have decided in your heart to give, not reluctantly or under compulsion, for God loves a cheerful giver." 2 Corinthians 9:7

**CONSIDER:**
1. What can you learn from the example of giving set by God the Father and His Son, Jesus?

2. Consider your motivation in giving. How could you give with purpose and being rooted in love?

3. List ways to give thoughtfully by leaning into relationship.

4. What might God be calling you to sacrifice in order to give more generously?

5. How will you plan ahead to give intentionally this Christmas?

# Way 9- You:

# Pursue Peace

"On that day, when evening had come, he said to them, 'Let us go across to the other side.' And leaving the crowd, they took him with them in the boat, just as he was. And other boats were with him. And a great windstorm arose, and the waves were breaking into the boat, so that the boat was already filling. But he was in the stern, asleep on the cushion.

And they woke him and said to him, 'Teacher, do you not care that we are perishing?' And he awoke and rebuked the wind and said to the sea, 'Peace! Be still!' And the wind ceased, and there was a great calm. He said to them, 'Why are you so afraid? Have you still no faith?' And they were filled with great fear and said to one another, 'Who then is this, that even the wind and the sea obey him?'" Mark 4:35-41 (ESV)

The holidays can bring complete chaos into our lives. Sometimes we create our own turmoil, but other times it is thrust upon us. In the middle of it all, it's easy for us to wonder or even question like the disciples did. Where is Jesus? Is He asleep while I am being pounded by life? Does Jesus even care that everything is falling apart?

Jesus did calm the storm that was raging around the boat, but then He confronted His disciples about their fear and lack of faith. These men had been walking with Jesus for a while. They had seen and participated in His miracles, and yet they did not trust His care for them. Referring to Jesus, Ephesians 2:14 says, "For he himself is our peace." You see, Peace Himself, was with the disciples in the boat, but they allowed the storm on the outside to create angst on the inside.

God works in different ways at different times. Sometimes Jesus calms the storms in our lives when we cry out to Him. But other times, He wants us to experience the peace that He brings to our souls despite our external circumstances. We cannot anticipate how He will work in our situations but we can expect it will be good.

In John 14:27 Jesus said, "Peace I leave with you; my peace I give you. I do not give to you as the world gives. Do not let your hearts be troubled and do not be afraid."

The world's pattern tells us that peace exists when life is quiet and calm and free from difficulty. Thank God that Jesus does not give peace as the world defines it! When our minds are renewed, we can have peace even in chaos. Peace the world offers is temporary and circumstantial; it relies on our physical, emotional, and mental state of being. But the peace Jesus brings is eternal; it operates on a spiritual level that transcends our circumstances, thoughts, and feelings. Peace is the Presence of Jesus not the absence of problems.

### The Promise of Peace

Based on Old Testament prophecy, the Jews had long awaited the coming Messiah who they believed would bring political and social peace. They rejected Jesus because that is not what He came to do. His purpose was to bring eternal, spiritual peace between God and humanity.

"As he approached Jerusalem and saw the city, he wept over it and said, 'If you, even you, had only known on this day

## Way 9- You: Pursue Peace

what would bring you peace—but now it is hidden from your eyes.'" Luke 19:41-42

Jesus wept over the hard-hearted misunderstanding of God's people. They could not see the real peace Jesus came to bring because they were blinded by their expectation of what peace should look like.

In a similar way, flawed thinking kept me from understanding and experiencing the peace that Jesus brings. I had been taught that God promises peace. So during times in my life when I didn't feel peace, I questioned God. "You promise peace, so why am I not feeling so very peaceful right now? Why am I angry or agitated or anxious? Why aren't You keeping Your promise?"

Some of my misunderstanding was rooted in the false doctrine of a problem-free Christian life, which caused me to believe that peace is circumstantial. That teaching is simply not Biblical. In John 16:33 Jesus said, "I have told you these things, so that in me you may have peace. In this world you will have trouble. But take heart! I have overcome the world." The peace Jesus is talking about is not a result of a life without turmoil. This is peace that only comes from knowing that God is in control.

I was also mistaken in believing that the promises of God are automatic. While His love for us is unconditional, sometimes His promises may require action on our part. Isaiah 26:3 (ESV) says, "You keep him in perfect peace whose mind is stayed on you, because he trusts in you."

The truth is, I do not have peace when I am more concerned about the fact that I am not in control than the truth that God is in control. I do not have peace when my mind is focused on my circumstances instead of my eyes being fixed on my Savior. If I'm honest, when I don't have peace, it is a symptom of not trusting God, of not being fully persuaded that He has a good plan and that His purpose will prevail.

# 12 Ways of Christmas

As I have grown to understand the Biblical definition of peace, I realize my own responsibility in the process. God does promise peace, but He wants us to join Him, to actively participate in cultivating peace.

### What does it look like to Pursue Peace?

First Peter 3:11b says "Seek peace and pursue it." To *Pursue Peace* means to earnestly desire, search for, and chase after spiritual wholeness. Like joy, peace is a fruit of the Spirit that is developed as we partner with God and allow it to flourish in our lives.

PURSUE PEACE IN YOUR HEART:
 ***Do not be anxious.** Pursuing peace at Christmas is not as easy as mind over matter. To not be overcome by anxiety at the holidays takes more than willpower. Thankfully, God gives us wisdom in His Word.

"Do not be anxious about anything, but in every situation, by prayer and petition, with thanksgiving, present your requests to God. And the peace of God, which transcends all understanding, will guard your hearts and your minds in Christ Jesus." Philippians 4:6-7

These verses start out, "Do not be anxious about anything." I am so grateful it did not stop there. God does not ask us to deny or ignore our struggles. The Scripture continues by telling us what to do instead of being anxious.

"But in every situation, by prayer and petition..." Now, Paul, who wrote Philippians, used a lot of words, and sometimes, when his letters have a list of what appear to be synonyms, we may be tempted to skim over them. But his word choice was intentional when he said by "prayer and petition." I'm no Greek scholar, but I do know how to look things up. The word translated *prayer* here means *exchange of wishes, earnest prayer*. The word for *petition* means *need*

## Way 9- You: Pursue Peace

*or entreaty.* You see, God wants us to tell Him everything, both what we want and what we need. Big or small, what matters to us matters to Him. He already knows our concerns, but He wants us to tell Him.

Sometimes little issues arise that I don't want to bother God with, so I try to just handle them on my own. It's like saying, "I've got this God; you go ahead and take care of the big stuff." But the weight of even those seemingly small things can add up to a heavy load. Instead of obsessing and stressing about the minutia of our seasons and celebrations, we can bring those requests to God. All of our holiday concerns, no matter how insignificant they feel, are part of "everything" God wants us to talk to Him about.

The third thing on Paul's list of what to do instead of being anxious is "thanksgiving." We already discussed gratitude in *Way 6: Choose Joy*, but this concept bears repeating. Expressing thanks to God for the blessings He has given us shifts our focus from our difficult circumstances. It places our attention on the good things in our lives and the Giver of every good and perfect gift.

After "present your requests to God," *then* comes the promise of peace. And it's not just any peace; this peace transcends understanding. God's peace goes beyond what we can comprehend because our earthly circumstances do not warrant it, but our eternal outcome does.

And what does that peace do? It brings Isaiah 26:3 full circle. When we keep our minds set on God and trust Him—through prayer, petition, thanksgiving—He brings us perfect peace. His peace, beyond human understanding, guards our hearts and minds.

**\*Think about such things.** Peace in our hearts is not an automatic outcome. We have to go after peace, grab hold of it, and guard it. Right after our "Do not be anxious" verses above, Paul said this:

# 12 Ways of Christmas

"Finally, brothers and sisters, whatever is true, whatever is noble, whatever is right, whatever is pure, whatever is lovely, whatever is admirable—if anything is excellent or praiseworthy—think about such things. Whatever you have learned or received or heard from me, or seen in me—put it into practice. And the God of peace will be with you." Philippians 4:8-9

Where we read above "think about such things," some translations say "dwell on these things." The word *dwell* is most often used in the context of living in a certain place. You see, processing and addressing our struggles is a good thing, but we can't live there. We need to move forward by fixing our minds on the goodness of God in order to maintain peace.

Paul's list of things to think about reminds us that our thought life has a direct effect on the condition of our hearts and minds. An indispensable part of a renewed mind is choosing to think about the right things. This may come as a revelation to you as it did to me—we get to choose what we think. We do not have to entertain every thought that pops into our minds. Instead, we have the power to cast down negative thoughts and replace them with thoughts that are honoring to God.

One of my favorite mechanisms for choosing my thoughts well is to fill my mind with the truth of God's Word. Studying and memorizing Scripture allows us to shift our mindset. It gives us a storehouse of right thoughts to turn to when wrong thoughts threaten to steal our peace.

When I have a specific need or concern, I often like to choose a go-to verse that applies to my circumstances. I'll post that verse on the mirror, on my refrigerator, and on a notecard to keep in my pocket during the day and under my pillow at night. When anxious thoughts or feelings arise, I grab that verse and literally hold on to the Word of God.

# Way 9- You: Pursue Peace

PURSUE PEACE WITH OTHERS:
**\*Be a peacemaker.** "Blessed are the peacemakers, for they will be called children of God." Matthew 5:9

The word *peacemaker* may stir up thoughts of weakness. Perhaps we imagine someone who is passive, timid, afraid to speak up, and allows others to take advantage of them. That's not how the Bible defines it. A peacemaker is one who displays strength in restraint and self-control. She does not stir up conflict by indulging in gossip or thriving on drama. A peacemaker is not a doormat. This is a person who keeps the peace, not by remaining silent when something needs to be said, but by speaking the truth in love.

A peacemaker is not simply one who is calm and quiet; she actively promotes peace and is a carrier of that peace to those around her. Being a peacemaker is remembering that peace is a gift from God, given to us through Jesus Christ so that we can in turn bring that gift to others.

**\*Live at peace.** "If it is possible, as far as it depends on you, live at peace with everyone." Romans 12:18

We've talked a little bit about preparing our hearts for complicated situations and people. The verse above reminds us that it is not always within our power to live peacefully with others. Please understand that a difficult person is not the same as a toxic person, nor is how to deal with them the same. With a difficult person, we can learn to tolerate them, manage our interactions, and set boundaries. But it may be impossible to live at peace with a toxic person because of their unhealthy behavior. Physical abuse, ongoing emotional, mental, and spiritual mistreatment without genuine repentance cannot be tolerated. While the Bible does tell us to forgive, it does not tell us to give unfettered excuse to unapologetic people who harm us and those we love. You can fully forgive someone, yet not allow them to have access to your life.

I don't have the time or expertise to flesh out the difference between a toxic and difficult person here, but if you need help

# 12 Ways of Christmas

with discerning the appropriate response in your particular situation, please seek the wisdom of a spiritual leader or professional counselor.

I make every effort to be transparent with you, friends. I know that God often uses the hard situations in our lives to bring hope to others. At the same time, my stories are not mine alone. Where they intersect with the lives of others, I want to be respectful of those people. While I will not tell you specifics of the situation, do I want to tell you about the goodness of my God. My husband made the difficult decision to remove a toxic person from our lives several years ago, and I fully support that. While we would still love and care and pray for that person, we could no longer allow them to poison our lives or the lives of our loved ones. That decision was a contributing factor to our peace at Christmas.

The verses surrounding Romans 12:18 give us context to understand what does depend on us when it comes to living at peace with others. Verse 17 says "Do not repay evil for evil," and verse 19 "Do not take revenge." These commands go back to the idea of being a peacemaker. We cannot dictate the way other people behave, but we can decide how we will respond.

***Choose your thoughts.** In *Choose Joy*, we talked about limiting our time with people who deplete us. Some people are simply unpleasant to be around. We don't necessarily have a reason to cut them out of our lives altogether, but they aren't the kind of people with whom we enjoy spending time or who we want to influence our lives. While another person's actions are out of our control, our reactions are our responsibility. Living at peace with others starts by looking at our own hearts.

"A good man brings good things out of the good stored up in his heart, and an evil man brings evil things out of the evil stored up in his heart. For the mouth speaks what the heart is full of." Luke 6:45

# Way 9- You: Pursue Peace

How we treat others will be determined by how we think about them. We cannot expect to speak kindly to someone who we constantly think ill of. When we focus on another person's faults and failures we are more likely to treat them with disrespect. Instead of dreading interactions at the holidays and milling over past offenses, we can choose better thoughts. By now you may have guessed that I practice this by employing a list. Sometimes I add an item or two to my gratitude list. But when I have found myself especially anxious over interacting with a specific person, I made an entire "think about such things" list where I stated every good thing I could come up with about that particular person. When I meditate on the positive things about others, I lead with grace, mercy, and love. This brings peace to my heart and my relationships.

Allow the Presence of Jesus to bring peace into the chaos this Christmas. Partner with Him in cultivating that peace and bringing it to others.

**PRAY:**
*Lord, thank You for Your promise of perfect peace that passes understanding. I know this promise comes with action on my part. May I chase after the peace You provide. Help me to set my mind on You because I trust You. Guide me into choosing thoughts that cultivate peace and casting down thoughts that stir up stress. Let me be a carrier of Your peace to those around me. In Jesus' name, amen.*

**MEDITATE OR MEMORIZE:**
"You keep him in perfect peace whose mind is stayed on you, because he trusts in you." Isaiah 26:3 (ESV)

# 12 Ways of Christmas

"Do not be anxious about anything, but in every situation, by prayer and petition, with thanksgiving, present your requests to God. And the peace of God, which transcends all understanding, will guard your hearts and your minds in Christ Jesus. Finally, brothers and sisters, whatever is true, whatever is noble, whatever is right, whatever is pure, whatever is lovely, whatever is admirable—if anything is excellent or praiseworthy—think about such things. Whatever you have learned or received or heard from me, or seen in me—put it into practice. And the God of peace will be with you." Philippians 4:6-9

**CONSIDER:**
1. How is the peace that Jesus offers different from the world's definition of peace?

2. Are there misconceptions you have had about peace?

3. What does God's Word say to do instead of being anxious?

4. How can you actively choose your thoughts and "think about such things?"

5. What would it mean for you to pursue peace with others?

# Way 10- Jesus:

# Surrender to Him

"This is how the birth of Jesus the Messiah came about: His mother Mary was pledged to be married to Joseph, but before they came together, she was found to be pregnant through the Holy Spirit. Because Joseph her husband was faithful to the law, and yet did not want to expose her to public disgrace, he had in mind to divorce her quietly.

But after he had considered this, an angel of the Lord appeared to him in a dream and said, 'Joseph son of David, do not be afraid to take Mary home as your wife, because what is conceived in her is from the Holy Spirit. She will give birth to a son, and you are to give him the name Jesus, because he will save his people from their sins.'

All this took place to fulfill what the Lord had said through the prophet: 'The virgin will conceive and give birth to a son, and they will call him Immanuel' (which means "God with us").

When Joseph woke up, he did what the angel of the Lord had commanded him and took Mary home as his wife." Matthew 1:18-24

As we approach Christmas, we so often talk about Mary and the honor she received as God chose her to be the mother of Jesus. We highlight the way Mary submitted to God's will. When the angel had appeared to her saying she would give birth to the Messiah, we see her surrendered response recorded in Luke 1:38. "'I am the Lord's servant,' Mary answered. 'May your word to me be fulfilled.'"

Sometimes, in focusing on Mary in the Christmas story, we forget about Joseph. We think of him as an extra or at best, a supporting actor and do not give enough credit to his role in the events that transpired. Joseph, too, was chosen by God, ordained to be the man who would raise His only Son on earth. I have no doubt that Mary and Joseph were literally a match made in Heaven.

Joseph had a plan for his life, and he had started to move forward with it when he became engaged to a girl named Mary. Joseph's plan did not include marrying his fiancé who showed up pregnant with a child he knew was not his. But Joe was an honorable man. He didn't want to make a public spectacle of Mary, so he decided on a discreet separation.

God sent an angel to explain the situation, and my favorite part of this passage is in the last verse. "When Joseph woke up, he did what the angel of the Lord had commanded him." Joseph didn't ask a bunch of questions or take time to mill it over. He didn't vaguebook for advice "Would you go through with a marriage to a girl who was pregnant with God's Son? Asking for a friend." Nope. Joseph woke up and did what he was told. His response was immediate, unconditional obedience, unfettered submission to God's plan.

This wasn't a one-time reaction for Joseph; he lived a lifestyle of surrender to God. We see another example of that after the visit of the Magi in Matthew 2:13-14. "When they had gone, an angel of the Lord appeared to Joseph in a dream. 'Get up,' he said, 'take the child and his mother and escape to Egypt. Stay there until I tell you, for Herod is going to search for the child to kill him.' So he got up, took the child and his mother during the night and left for Egypt." This time, Joseph

## Way 10- Jesus: Surrender to Him

didn't even wait until the morning. He got up right then, in the middle of the night, and did exactly as the angel had said.

Friends, if we want to cultivate a restful season, we need to follow the example of Jesus' parents, and submit to God's perfect will. Surrender was not only their lifestyle; it was their first response. I need more of that in my life because, frankly, my reactions are often delayed despite having heard a thousand times, "Slow obedience is no obedience."

### A Christmas Message

My friend Kim was beaming when she told me the news. She had recommended that I be the guest speaker at her church's annual Christmas Tea. Nothing was certain, but just the prospect was a big deal for me. When my first book was released a few months earlier, I felt like my ministry was beginning to move forward, and I started receiving invitations to speak. This event could be my second official speaking engagement.

As I began to pray about the opportunity, I felt led to start preparing right away without being sure of an invitation. You need to know this, I am driven by productivity. I hate wasting time, especially when there are other things I should be doing. Because I knew in my spirit I needed to write this talk, I hoped that was confirmation the event would happen.

My message was nearly complete, and I was feeling good about presenting it by the first week of December when I received the call that I would not be invited to speak at the Christmas Tea. The organizers did graciously promise to keep me in mind for future events.

In the past, I would have reacted poorly to such a notification, regarding it as rejection. I would have questioned God and wondered if I never heard from Him in the first place. I may have even been angry with my friend for getting my hopes up and considered giving up speaking altogether. But

## 12 Ways of Christmas

this time was different. I believed I had been led by the Spirit, and I trusted that God doesn't want to waste my time any more than I do.

It is okay to be disappointed. However, we cannot let disappointment cause us to become discouraged. I had to process that what I had planned, what I had hoped for, what I thought God was leading me toward did not happen. Still, I had assurance in my obedience. I had come to understand that when God asks us to do something, the outcome isn't always what we expect. But where the Holy Spirit leads, there is indeed a purpose. Like I mentioned, this would have only been my second time delivering a full-length message. I definitely needed practice writing and presenting a talk, so I was able to view all the work I had done as preparation.

The following week I had a regularly scheduled check-in with my friend Hanna who is also a writer and speaker. She and I had an agreement to encourage each other in our callings, share progress on our projects, and provide accountability for our goals. She knew I had been developing my talk and looking forward to the event, so she shared in my disappointment. But Hanna encouraged me that the message would go to good use because surely, some year I would speak at Christmastime.

Let me encourage you. Sometimes things don't work out the way we planned, even after we've prayed through and felt certain we're walking in step with the Spirit. When the result does not look like we had hoped, that doesn't mean we did not hear from God. Sometimes in the disappointment, He is teaching us a lesson, building our character, or preparing us for something else.

I rarely have a telephone conversation unless it has been scheduled in advance. So it was odd when my cell rang that Wednesday morning in December, and an unknown number showed up on the caller ID. It was a woman I had never met,

# Way 10- Jesus: Surrender to Him

the relative of an acquaintance, that had read my book. She invited me to speak the following week at an appreciation breakfast honoring women who serve in a local Bible study community.

Look, I know that most local church pastors get up every single week and preach a new sermon. That's awesome. But I was brand new, so one week would not have been enough time for me to write and prepare to speak a message. However, I was already equipped with a talk to deliver and was, therefore, able to say "Yes," to the opportunity. This only happened because I was led by the Spirit and submitted to God's plan. While we won't always know the outcome, we can trust that surrender to Him will turn out for our good and God's glory every time.

**What does it look like to Surrender to Him?**

To *Surrender to Him* is letting go of our own desires, our struggle to be in control, and trusting God with our lives. This is the practical application of not only asking Jesus to be our Savior but making Him our Lord.

Jesus told us what surrender looks like when He gave us the Lord's Prayer.

> "This, then, is how you should pray:
> 'Our Father in heaven,
> hallowed be your name,
> your kingdom come,
> your will be done,
> on earth as it is in heaven.'"
> Matthew 6:9-10

But Jesus didn't just tell us, He showed us what surrender looks like by living a lifestyle of surrender throughout His time on earth. Jesus' life was marked by submission to the will of the Father. John 6:38 quotes Him, "For I have come down from heaven not to do my will but to do the will of him who sent me."

"Your will be done" is not only how we should pray, but how we should live.

Jesus set the ultimate example of surrender in the garden of Gethsemane. Moments before His arrest that would lead to His crucifixion, Jesus put into practice the prayer He had taught. Jesus' submission was revealed not only in His words and the position of His body but so much more so in the posture of His heart.

"Going a little farther, he fell with his face to the ground and prayed, 'My Father, if it is possible, may this cup be taken from me. Yet not as I will, but as you will.'" Matthew 26:39

Jesus, being fully God and fully man, was completely aware of all the suffering He would experience. This knowledge filled Him with "sorrow to the point of death."

Jesus knew with God all things are possible. He also knew the plan from the beginning was that He, the spotless Lamb of God, would be the sacrifice to atone for the sins of the world. While His human nature may have been averse to suffering, Jesus fully surrendered the will of His flesh to the will of His Father.

At this moment in the garden, Jesus modeled the relationship that we too are able to have with our Father. We can have intimate communication with God, speaking to Him freely and openly about our sorrows and desires. But Jesus' entire prayer hinges on the small but weighty word, *yet*. Despite our internal struggles, surrender gives God's will the final word.

When we are fully submitted to God and our hearts are in alignment with His heart, His will becomes our will. Surrender is more than a one-time decision to follow Jesus. It

# Way 10- Jesus: Surrender to Him

is a daily commitment to living a lifestyle of "Your will be done."

SURRENDER YOUR PLANS:
"Many plans are in a person's heart, but it is the Lord's purpose that prevails." Proverbs 19:21

I begin planning for the next Christmas before the tree is even up the previous year. I love to dream of what may be and think through the steps of how to get there. Look, God is not opposed to the making of plans. In fact, it is a vital part of being a good steward of our resources. In Luke 14, Jesus talks about being ready for what is to come by counting the cost. And Proverbs 6:6-8 tells us to consider the ant who "stores its provisions in summer and gathers its food at harvest" in preparation for the days ahead.

If we don't make some advanced arrangements, how will we know when and where we will gather, what we will eat, and who will be coming for dinner? Without a plan, the holidays would be utter chaos. On the other hand, when we hold on to our own plans too tightly, they become an idol, and we fall apart when things don't go our way. Between the two extremes, there is a balance that is honoring to God.

The solution is not to ditch our plans altogether and let the holidays unfold however they will. But rather than developing our own plans and asking God to bless them, we need to actively seek out His plans.

You see, God already has a plan for our lives. He's had it from before the beginning of time. Jeremiah 29:11 may be a familiar verse, but The Message paraphrase strikes me with fresh understanding. It reads, "I know what I'm doing. I have it all planned out—plans to take care of you, not abandon you, plans to give you the future you hope for."

God's plans aren't just good plans, they are the best plans. That's right, God's plans are the best plans. I emphasize this because I'm always aware that God has a good plan. But often, I behave as though His plan is more a starting point before I offer my input on how the plan could be improved. I forget that since God is sovereign, He doesn't need my suggestions. The pattern of the world is to cling to our own plans. A renewed mind trusts in God's perfect plan.

"Commit to the LORD whatever you do, and he will establish your plans." Proverbs 16:3

Seeking God's plan for the holidays starts by talking to Him first and asking Him to help us accomplish His will. Now, I don't ask God whether we should meet at 5:30 or 6:00. But I do ask that He helps us to find a time that fits everyone's schedule. I wouldn't ask if we should have turkey or ham, but I could ask God to help me be a good steward as I plan the menu. These seem like small things, but we already covered how God wants us to talk to Him about everything. What matters to us truly does matter to Him.

SURRENDER YOUR NEED TO KNOW:

I am detail-oriented; my husband is a "big picture" guy. Most of the time, these differences mean we work well together as we balance each other out. I keep Chris from missing small but important elements he may have overlooked. He keeps me moving forward, not getting caught up in the minutia.

I ask a lot of questions. That can be frustrating to my husband who processes things differently than I do. Sometimes, my questions are for clarification, so I know what my next step is. But, to be honest, sometimes my asking is to not seek understanding, but to debate the course of action.

I do the same thing to God. Now, asking God questions to understand is not wrong. Proverbs tells us to get understanding, and James says if you lack wisdom, ask God who gives generously.

While I want to believe my motivation in inquiring of God is to understand so that I can be obedient, often, I'm actually questioning whether God knows what He's doing. When we

## Way 10- Jesus: Surrender to Him

ask questions of God, we need to examine our hearts. It is an important distinction to determine whether we are asking questions for clarification or if we are questioning God's sovereignty.

Our Father is both God of the details and of the big picture. I don't have to make sure He hasn't forgotten something. And for those of you who are focused on the end goal, you don't have to keep Him moving; His timing is perfect.

In the Gospel of John, Jesus had a long conversation with His disciples explaining things to come—His betrayal, Peter's denial, the persecution they would endure, and the gift of the Holy Spirit. But in chapter 16 verse 12, He told them, "I have much more to say to you, more than you can now bear." Sometimes God tells us things on a "need to know basis." He fully understands the limitations of human minds and emotions; He knows what we can handle. God makes His will known to us when the time is right, but He wants most of all for us to learn to trust Him.

We see this kind of trust displayed by Abram in Genesis 12. God told him to leave his country and his people and go "to a place I will show you." Then, Scripture says, "So Abram went, as the Lord had told him." We cannot miss the fact that this man left behind everyone and everything he had known and headed for an undisclosed location.

Surrender so often looks like stepping out in faith before we see the entire path forward. Living a life fully surrendered to God does not mean we cannot ask questions. But it does mean that when we do not get the answers we are looking for, we still trust Him. I'm not there yet, but I want my story to read like Abram's. "God said, 'Go'…so Cassia went."

SURRENDER YOUR EXPECTATIONS:

Expectations are thieves of our joy and peace. I had built up in my mind an image of the perfect Christmas. But year after year, my unrealistic anticipation led to unmet

# 12 Ways of Christmas

expectations that left me miserable when the holidays were over. Surrender relies heavily on flexibility. It's not true surrender when we are too rigid to adjust when necessary. Even when we have carefully prayed through our plans, the unexpected often prevents life from happening exactly the way we anticipated. Hold on loosely to your plans this Christmas.

On "Our First Best Christmas," I surrendered all of my expectations—of the perfect meal, a perfectly clean and decorated house, finding the perfect gift. I exchanged my expectations for trust that God is good, that He cares about me and what is important to me. He is in control even when everything feels out of control. The Lord's purpose will prevail. No matter what happens, it will work out for our good and His glory.

**PRAY:**
*Our Father in Heaven, hallowed be Your name, Your kingdom come, Your will be done, on earth as it is in Heaven. Lord, I want to live a life fully surrendered to You. Please teach me to seek out Your plans and to hold on loosely to my own plans. May I learn to fully trust in Your goodness. In Jesus' name, amen.*

**MEDITATE OR MEMORIZE:**
"This, then, is how you should pray: 'Our Father in heaven, hallowed be your name, your kingdom come, your will be done, on earth as it is in heaven.'" Matthew 6:9-10

"Many plans are in a person's heart, but it is the Lord's purpose that prevails." Proverbs 19:21

# Way 10- Jesus: Surrender to Him

"For I know the plans I have for you," declares the LORD, "plans to prosper you and not to harm you, plans to give you hope and a future." Jeremiah 29:11

**CONSIDER:**

1. How do Joseph, Mary, Jesus, and Abram inspire you to live a surrendered life?

2. In what way can "Your will be done" become not only a prayer but a lifestyle?

3. How it is possible to balance surrendering your holiday plans without failing to plan at all?

4. Why is it often more difficult to surrender to what you don't fully understand?

5. What expectations do you need to surrender to God this Christmas?

# Way 11- Others:

# Serve Selflessly

"Six days before the Passover, Jesus came to Bethany, where Lazarus lived, whom Jesus had raised from the dead. Here a dinner was given in Jesus' honor. Martha served, while Lazarus was among those reclining at the table with him. Then Mary took about a pint of pure nard, an expensive perfume; she poured it on Jesus' feet and wiped his feet with her hair. And the house was filled with the fragrance of the perfume.

But one of his disciples, Judas Iscariot, who was later to betray him, objected, 'Why wasn't this perfume sold and the money given to the poor? It was worth a year's wages.' He did not say this because he cared about the poor but because he was a thief; as keeper of the money bag, he used to help himself to what was put into it.

'Leave her alone,' Jesus replied. 'It was intended that she should save this perfume for the day of my burial. You will always have the poor among you, but you will not always have me.'" John 12:1-8

Back in *Way 2: Be Present*, our first chapter about loving others well, we were introduced to our friend Martha and her sister Mary. Here, we encounter the sisters again at another dinner party given in honor of Jesus.

# 12 Ways of Christmas

Remember the first time we met Martha? She asked Jesus, "Lord, don't you care that my sister has left me to do all the work by myself? Tell her to help me!" Then Jesus called Martha out for being worried about everything except the one thing that truly matters.

Maybe that cautionary tale makes us think we should stop serving altogether so we can be present during the holidays. But let's look back closely at what happened in the previous scene. Jesus did not correct Martha for serving. He didn't say anything to her until she started to complain. Jesus was speaking to Martha's heart—her attitude about service, her expectations of others, and her inability to find a balance. She was worried about what everyone else was doing and was motivated by accomplishment.

We do not know for sure how the relationship developed, but the next time we see this family in Scripture, they had become close friends with Jesus. When their brother, Lazarus took ill, the sisters sent word to Jesus, "Lord, the one you love is sick." John 11:5 says, "Now Jesus loved Martha and her sister and Lazarus."

In what seemed to be an unexpected turn of events, Lazarus died before Jesus arrived. But we see how that situation had turned around in the passage at the beginning of this chapter. This dinner in Jesus' honor was likely to celebrate that He had raised Lazarus from the dead.

In his Gospel account, John makes no commentary on Martha's attitude; he simply said, "Martha served." And Jesus did not correct her this time around. The Bible doesn't elaborate, but I believe that here, we see a transformed Martha. Jesus did not change Martha's personality; He changed her heart. She still served, no longer driven by productivity, but motivated by love.

At the first dinner, Martha served the food. At the second dinner, she served Jesus.

# Way 11- Others: Serve Selflessly

Now, Martha was a footnote in this passage. Let's not miss the point of this story. At the first dinner, we see Mary sitting at Jesus' feet listening intently. This time, Mary was present with Jesus, and she also served Him. In fact, Judas criticized Mary because the perfume she used was very expensive, and he considered it a waste. Jesus did not correct the servant, but the one who did not recognize the value in her act of service.

Practically speaking, how does serving make the holidays more restful and less stressful? Isn't that just one more thing to add to our never-ending list? Serving is not counter to being present with others or caring for ourselves. But in all these things, we need moderation that brings balance. Mary's service to Jesus reminds us that we can be present with others and experience joy, not in spite of service, but through service.

**Transformed Service**

Serving is important to me. Not just because I identify with Martha, but because in studying Scripture, I have seen that Jesus set the example of serving and asks us to follow it. (And, that reassures me—since I'm like Martha.) Much like He did with Martha, Jesus changed my heart and not my personality. In my many failed attempts at the perfect Christmas, my error was not *that* I served, but my focus in serving. I valued productivity over people. While I was convinced I was toiling away to make the holidays special for everyone else, all my activity was self-focused.

Between the years of slamming around in the kitchen and "Our First Best Christmas" there were small, incremental changes. I gradually learned to love others well while serving and still prioritizing being present. Rather than finding my identity in service, I became fully rooted in who I am in Christ. My service was transformed into an outpouring of love for others because He first loved me.

# 12 Ways of Christmas

After we relocated a state away from what had always been home, I wondered what Christmas would look like. Our larger family celebrations would no longer be at our house. Could the holidays feel full if I wasn't serving?

For 20 years, we had rushed to gather with extended family on my side until late on Christmas Eve and on my husband's side early Christmas Day. But that year, since we would have to travel several hours to those celebrations, we scheduled them away from the 25th, so we could be at home on Christmas morning. Those two days provided our most intimate and intentional holiday experience yet.

Besides weddings and funerals, Chris, Asa, and I rarely get "dressed up" to go somewhere together. But a candlelight Christmas Eve service was the perfect occasion. After church, we sat down for juicy steaks at a local favorite. Back at home, warm homemade apple crisp was waiting to be topped with vanilla bean ice cream. Although he has received the same two gifts every year for his entire life—a movie and pajamas—Asa was surprised by his Christmas Eve presents. The evening came to a close with us snuggled under piles of fleece to watch holiday classics by the light of the Christmas tree.

The next morning, steam rolled from the tops of blueberry muffins as I retrieved them from the oven. I heard my husband whisper in the other room, "Asa, it's Christmas! Time to get up!" We opened gifts one at a time, tried on our new clothes, and tried out our new gadgets. By the time we were finished, the roast was cooked through, and a few favorite side dishes were placed around it on the farmhouse table.

Planning an intimate celebration and creating new traditions was not less important than hosting a large family gathering. That year, the two people in my own home, who were for many years overlooked as I focused on everyone and everything else at Christmas, were the center of my service. I discovered another level of choosing better, serving while being present.

# Way 11- Others: Serve Selflessly

**What does it look like to Serve Others Selflessly?**

To *Serve Selflessly* means to minister to others, honoring their needs above our own. Service is an outward expression of love. We love well when we think less of ourselves and more of others.

Maybe you've heard the saying, "Live like you are dying." I don't know what comes to your mind when you hear those words. I immediately start humming that Tim McGraw song. The things on his list—sky diving, mountain climbing, bull riding—those don't really resonate with me.

You know what Jesus did knowing His death was coming soon? Jesus humbled Himself in an act of service, washing the feet of His twelve disciples, including one who would deny Him and another who would betray Him. And here is how He said we ought to follow His example:

"Whoever wants to become great among you must be your servant, and whoever wants to be first must be your slave—just as the Son of Man did not come to be served, but to serve, and to give his life as a ransom for many." Matthew 20:26b-28

Not everyone is like me and Martha. But regardless of our personalities, all Jesus followers are commissioned to heed His example and serve others selflessly. Specific acts of service will look different for each of us depending on our gifts, personalities, resources, and the people we have been called to serve. But the heart with which we all serve should be to live like Jesus.

SERVE WITH THE RIGHT ATTITUDE:
"Do nothing out of selfish ambition or vain conceit. Rather, in humility value others above yourselves, not looking to your own interests but each of you to the interests of the others. In your relationships with one another, have the same

mindset as Christ Jesus: Who, being in very nature God, did not consider equality with God something to be used to his own advantage; rather, he made himself nothing by taking the very nature of a servant, being made in human likeness." Philippians 2:3-7

It's easy to choose our holiday undertakings based on what's in it for us. Even what we claim to be doing for the good of others can be focused on how we want to serve, not how others need to be served. Paul reminded the Philippians that nothing we do should be self-seeking or driven by empty pride. We cannot esteem ourselves as better than anyone else or criticize the people we serve. We must not grumble, complain, or boast about our service.

Friends, I'm so grateful the Bible is not just a list of what not to do. Verse three starts out telling us about the wrong attitude, but Paul immediately follows up with what we should do instead.

Selfless service requires humility. Jesus, God incarnate, made Himself nothing and took on the role of the lowliest servant in order to demonstrate His love for us. The inward development of having the same mindset as Christ will manifest itself in the outward behavior of servanthood. We are invited to leave behind the self-serving pattern of the world and to choose a renewed mind that serves selflessly.

In Matthew 7:12 Jesus said, "So in everything, do to others what you would have them do to you." This is a direct parallel to "Love your neighbor as yourself." We could look at this verse as an admonition to consider how we would like to be served and serve others in that way. Thinking about our own desires is a good starting point, but it shouldn't be the end. I would love for someone to pitch in with sides and help with the dishes, but I would not be pleased if they reorganized my pantry. Selfless service is not just transferring our own desires onto others, but being intentional to serve people in a way that

## Way 11- Others: Serve Selflessly

blesses them. We will only know the wants and needs of others when we lean into relationship in order to discover how we can best serve.

SERVE WITHOUT EXPECTATION:
At the first dinner, Martha expected help from her sister. Girl, same. When it comes to holiday prep, what I think "needs" to be done is so very obvious, but my husband and son are oblivious. What is important to me is not the same as what is important to them. Before "Our First Best Christmas," I decided all the things I wanted to accomplish over the holidays and expected my family to jump into my plan. I did not bother to have a conversation about what I would ask of them or whether they wanted to participate. When I communicate the help I would like to have, they are often willing to assist me with many things. But I also have to let go of the expectation that they will do whatever I ask in the way I want it to be done. Because like Martha, I am often worried about many things that do not matter. While I can ask for help in serving, I cannot project my desires onto others and demand that they serve in the way I expect.

Martha also expected Jesus to notice all she was doing. That was me, too. In the past, I had put a lot of effort into our Christmas celebrations, and I thought everyone should take notice. My top love language is *Words of Affirmation*. It warms my soul to hear, "What a lovely gift; you must have spent a lot of time wrapping this package!" But the unfortunate truth is that much of what we do to serve during the holidays will go unnoticed by others. So we need to remember that while acknowledgment and gratitude are encouraging, they are not the reason why we serve. If I make an honest assessment, I don't notice everything everyone else does to serve me. The good news is, God gives us grace. He sees us. He notices every act of selfless service, even when it feels like no one else cares. We serve God by serving others; we serve others to point them to Him.

SERVE MOTIVATED BY LOVE:
"Above all, love each other deeply, because love covers over a multitude of sins. Offer hospitality to one another without grumbling. Each of you should use whatever gift you have received to serve others, as faithful stewards of God's grace in its various forms. If anyone speaks, they should do so as one who speaks the very words of God. If anyone serves, they should do so with the strength God provides, so that in all things God may be praised through Jesus Christ. To him be the glory and the power forever and ever. Amen." 1 Peter 4:8-11

Love is a verb. Service is love in action.

We have different reasons for all the activities we engage in at the holidays—self-focus, obligation, comparison, people-pleasing. What separates busy work from acts of service is our motivation. When we are motivated by love—love for God and love for others—serving becomes a joy rather than a chore. While we may be tempted to only count the big, overt demonstrations of meeting needs, when we understand serving to be an expression of love, even the small things become acts of service.

Peter points out two ways we can show love through serving—hospitality and using our unique gifts.

The year we moved, I dreamed of inviting all the neighbors over for a Christmas party. My husband reminded me of the reality of our situation. Our little log cabin on the creek is charming, but it was for sure a fixer-upper. At that time, there was barely room for the three inhabitants, and the place was definitely not suitable for company. Plus, while I am

## Way 11- Others: Serve Selflessly

obnoxiously extroverted, my guys would prefer that our home remain their sanctuary and not my entertaining space. I'm grateful for Jesus' example. He did not have a place to lay his head, but that didn't keep Him from being hospitable. Showing hospitality is not limited to inviting people to gather in your house around your dining room table. What a blessing if you are able to do that with joy. While not all of us can invite people into our homes, we can invite them into our lives. Hospitality is about intentionally making others feel welcome wherever we may be.

During the dinner at the start of this chapter, Mary did not serve in what we may consider to be the traditional way—by preparing the meal as her sister did. In Mark 14:8 Jesus said, "She has done what she could." Mary served Jesus from her heart with the resources she had. At this dinner, both sisters served Jesus in different ways according to their gifts and personalities. God has created each of us uniquely to serve in different ways. Your service may not look like mine, as Mary's didn't look like Martha's. Let's be careful not to compare our service to anyone else's, but to simply be obedient in how God has called us to serve.

Service is a way of life, having the same mindset as Christ by putting others' needs before our own. There will never be a shortage of opportunities to serve during the holidays. All the programs and special services and charitable outreaches mean more help is needed. Trying to do everything will lead to a more stressful season. As we continue to surrender our plans at Christmastime, we can ask God to reveal to us the good works that He has planned in advance for us to do. I'm grateful for Peter's encouragement to serve "with the strength God provides." We can't do it all during the holidays, but God will empower us to do everything that He asks us to do.

# 12 Ways of Christmas

**PRAY:**
*Oh Lord, please teach me to serve selflessly. Help me to lean into relationship with the people You have given me. When my attitude or expectations start to get in the way, help me to choose the right motivation and to serve others with love. In Jesus' name, amen.*

**MEDITATE OR MEMORIZE:**
"Whoever wants to become great among you must be your servant, and whoever wants to be first must be your slave—just as the Son of Man did not come to be served, but to serve, and to give his life as a ransom for many." Matthew 20:26b-28

"Do nothing out of selfish ambition or vain conceit. Rather, in humility value others above yourselves, not looking to your own interests but each of you to the interests of the others." Philippians 2:3-4

"Each of you should use whatever gift you have received to serve others, as faithful stewards of God's grace in its various forms." 1 Peter 4:10

**CONSIDER:**
1. How can you balance serving others with being present?

2. Give some examples of the right and wrong attitudes to have about serving.

3. What expectations have affected your service? How can you release them?

# Way 11- Others: Serve Selflessly

4. How would your service look different if it was motivated by love?

5. In what areas do you need to rely on God's strength to serve this Christmas?

# Way 12- You:

# Find Rest

"Thus the heavens and the earth were completed in all their vast array. By the seventh day God had finished the work he had been doing; so on the seventh day, he rested from all his work. Then God blessed the seventh day and made it holy, because on it he rested from all the work of creating that he had done." Genesis 2:1-3

For six days, the Creator worked, forming the entire Universe. And on the seventh day, He rested. God does not need rest, but He set an example for us of both work and rest. A rhythm. Humanity was given work to do from the very beginning, before the fall. Work is not punishment; it is part of our purpose as image-bearers. God worked, and being created in His image, we were also made to do work. God rested, and He designed us to rest as well. From the front cover of this book we have been talking about cultivating a restful season, that will only happen when we embrace the rest that God has given.

The message the world sends, and that I get caught up in at Christmas, is that it's all about the hustle and bustle. I love all the festivities and activities that happen during this time of year, but I wonder if I'm not the only one that falls into this idea that we have to do all things and be all the things. We so quickly become overscheduled and under-rested, convinced that somehow busyness equals fullness. A renewed mind is intentional to find rest throughout the season.

**Forced Rest**

I thought I knew what rest was. I had this chapter outlined and Scripture passages all picked out. But then, just a few weeks before I sat down to put my fingers to the keyboard for *Find Rest*, my doctor said this, "The only way your body will heal is with rest. If you do not rest, it will prolong your healing or cause permanent damage." My forced rest was the result of a head-on collision between my SUV and a left-of-center pick-up truck. But I have friends who have been forced to rest after a face-to-face reckoning between their relentless schedule and an impending health crisis.

We were made for a regular cadence of rest. When we continue to ignore that inherent need, we may not see the results immediately, but neglect will catch up with us eventually. The longer we wait to address the problem, the more permanent the damage may be.

In the past, I have often confused rest with laziness. I have gotten it wrong both ways. Sometimes I refused to rest, considering it slothful. Other times, I lounged about, counting it as rest. During the six weeks after the accident, I learned to listen to my body. Instead of pushing through like I normally would, I sat down when I was out of energy. I turned off the alarm clock and slept until my body was ready to be awake. I even napped on afternoons when it was needed.

In addition to bodily damage, the impact of the wreck left me needing healing for my mind and emotions. This would not happen if I filled every waking moment of my downtime with noise. So while I did disconnect with a chick-flick or two, rest for my whole self meant giving plenty of space for quiet and processing and prayer.

# Way 12- You: Find Rest

Now understand that, because of a traumatic incident, I needed intense, healing rest, not regular rest. But in this time of forced pause, I got to know myself more. I discovered areas I had over-filled with activity and learned to listen to my body for cues that I need a break. I finally understood that choosing to embrace rest does not inhibit my productivity. Rest is a gift that breathes more life into my times of work.

### What does it look like to Find Rest?

To *Find Rest* means to intentionally carve out space for renewal in your body, mind, and soul. The word *intentionally* is important here. Rest does not make time for itself. If we are not diligent in making rest a priority, we will quickly be overtaken by all of the other activities and obligations that mark the holidays.

You know what a margin is, right? Those white spaces on the outer edge of ruled notebook paper that indicate where not to write. Don't fill your life to the edges. We need empty spaces, time that is not consumed with toil and noise.

I wonder if you tell yourself the same lie I often have. "I'll rest when… When Christmas is over, when the decorations are put away, when we get through this season, then I'll rest." But life never slows down; the world keeps spinning at the same speed. Respite is something we need to do deliberately. At the holidays more than ever, we have to consciously choose rest, maybe even schedule it on our calendars.

It is not self-focused to care for yourself so you can function at your best. In fact, it is really unlikely that anyone else will do it for you. My husband can tell me what I ought to do, my friends can give encouragement, and my doctor can offer advice. But they cannot make changes for me. At the end of the day, I am responsible for my own well-being.

# 12 Ways of Christmas

Loving ourselves in a balanced way is not akin to the self-care that is the pattern of the world. Look, I'm up for a massage, mani-pedi, and a frou-frou coffee just about any day of the week. Those things are fun for a little pick-me-up. But they are shallow, exterior luxuries that are a poor substitution for genuine rest. Now, I'm not about to switch over at the end of this book and start writing a medical journal or wellness guide. But I cannot move on without the reminder that our bodies are the temple of the Holy Spirit. These tents are temporary, but God wants us to be good stewards of them while we're camping out.

FIND REST EVERY DAY:
 *Sleep. When we overload our schedules at Christmastime, something has to give. After our time with God, the next thing we usually let go of is sleep. I'm not much of a morning person. When I try to get out of bed an hour earlier to increase my productivity, I end up moving slower the entire day. But I also know that if I keep on working in the evening, at 10 pm I'll get a second wind. And a third at midnight. I think I'm pulling one over on time. In high school, I could easily stay up all night and own the next day with no lag for recovery. But the truth is, as I get older, I have come to realize that I cannot borrow from tomorrow. In the long run, without enough nighttime sleep, I am less productive and more cranky.

Psalm 127:2 (ESV) says, "It is in vain that you rise up early and go late to rest, eating the bread of anxious toil; for he gives to his beloved sleep."

God designed our physical bodies to require rest every day. All the research is out there and easy to find. Most of us know what we should do; we simply don't do it. While we recognize that the human body needs "adequate sleep," that magic number is different for each of us at different times in our lives and even during different seasons of the year. My husband runs well on 6 hours or so, but I have always needed to doze

## Way 12- You: Find Rest

for a minimum of 8 to 10 hours just to function. Maybe you've seen it on a T-shirt or as a meme: "Jesus took naps. Be like Jesus." Look, sometimes we need extra sleep. Knowing the right amount for you requires listening to your body and adapting your habits.

***Rest for your mind.** For years, I gave myself ample time for sleep, but I laid in bed all night tossing and turning. My doctor helped me to address some health issues, and make lifestyle changes. (And I also bought the world's best mattress.) But there was another factor in my struggle to sleep. I couldn't shut off my mind at night. Occasionally, I was worried or anxious, but not always.

As many writers will attest, some of my best ideas come when I should be sleeping. The perfect words formulate in the middle of the night. There are times when I promise to remember in the morning, but it never happens. If I don't write down my thoughts immediately, the words are lost forever. In one after-midnight session, words flowed like my backyard creek in high water. Afterward, I thanked God for the great insights from His Word that I could share with others. And I asked Him this question, "Why do you seem to save this inspiration for when I should be sleeping?" I felt like God answered, "Maybe you should be quiet more often."

I like to unwind in the evenings and binge-watch shows with my guys, but that is not rest for my mind. We need dedicated quiet time, mental space to process all of our happenings and decisions. As I free my mind from constant distraction and activity, my thoughts untangle naturally throughout the day instead of keeping me up all night. I also do a brain download before bedtime. When I review my calendar and list the things that need to be addressed the next day, they are no longer bouncing around in my head while I should be sleeping. In being still and practicing quietness, I find rest for my mind.

# 12 Ways of Christmas

FIND SABBATH REST:
"There are six days when you may work, but the seventh day is a day of sabbath rest, a day of sacred assembly. You are not to do any work; wherever you live, it is a sabbath to the Lord." Leviticus 23:3

In *Way 3: Prepare Your Heart,* we began to unpack God's appointed holy days found in Leviticus chapter 23. While many of the holy days include the command to "Do no regular work," the Sabbath was the only one to make God's "Top 10 List" when He etched the Commandments on stone tablets and instructed Moses to deliver them to His people. The Sabbath was a weekly day set aside for rest—to cease from work and to gather in sacred assembly.

**\*Gather in Community.** Part of observing the Sabbath was to come together in a sacred assembly. When I was a kid, we went to church twice on Sunday, every Wednesday night, and occasionally for special services or activities in between. A minister friend of mine said that today, the average church-goer only attends on-site service twice per month. Now, since most churches offer some sort of online resource, it's even easier to skip the crowd and watch a sermon from the comfort of your own couch. While it is convenient, online options are not intended to be a replacement for gathering, but an alternative when we cannot make it to church in person.

We were created for community. God established a weekly rhythm of gathering with other believers, so we could worship together and encourage one another. We find rest for our souls as we connect and engage with our brothers and sisters in Christ.

**\*Rest from Work.** When the Israelites were in the wilderness, God provided fresh food for them to gather daily. But on the day before the Sabbath, they could gather twice as much. In Exodus 16:23, we see that Moses instructed God's people on how to prepare in advance for their day of rest.

# Way 12- You: Find Rest

"This is what the LORD commanded: 'Tomorrow is to be a day of sabbath rest, a holy sabbath to the LORD. So bake what you want to bake and boil what you want to boil. Save whatever is left and keep it until morning.'"

Friend, this is good advice for us to follow during the holidays. Plan ahead for days of solemn rest. Bake what you want to bake; wrap what you want to wrap. Then set it aside so you are free to observe a holy Sabbath. While there is a need to make all the preparations, Christmas should be a time of celebration and a time to relax. Ceasing from work allows us to lean into relationship with God and others. This is not only rest for our bodies, being present in this way is rest for our souls.

"Remember the Sabbath day by keeping it holy. Six days you shall labor and do all your work, but the seventh day is a sabbath to the LORD your God. On it you shall not do any work, neither you, nor your son or daughter, nor your male or female servant, nor your animals, nor any foreigner residing in your towns. For in six days the LORD made the heavens and the earth, the sea, and all that is in them, but he rested on the seventh day. Therefore the LORD blessed the Sabbath day and made it holy." Exodus 20:8-11

God blessed the Sabbath. He sanctified it, set it apart on the seventh day of creation, before the fall, before the Mosaic law was presented in Exodus. The invitation to rest was presented in the first week of the earth's existence. It is a divine expression of our Father's favor that He gives us the reward of rest.

To cease from work doesn't necessarily mean to stop all activity. The Pharisees took this invitation to rest and turned it into a rule to be followed with impunity. They added a bunch of regulations that God had not given. The Sabbath is not a legalistic ritual to rule over us and make us feel guilty for working. It is not a punishment; rest is a benefit. It is not a burden; it's a blessing. Jesus set an example of rest in a balanced way. He did what was required, He did the work of the Lord, and He rested.

Jesus said in Mark 2:27 "The Sabbath was made for man, not man for the Sabbath." This holy day of rest is a gift to us, a time to be set apart for communion with our Creator. It has not been abolished, but Jesus redefined it. The Sabbath isn't about observing a specific day of the week in a prescribed way, but ceasing from work in order to enjoy the presence of the Lord. Sabbath is time set apart to rest from work and rest in God.

**\*Come to Jesus**: In my Bible, the words below are written in red, which indicates that they are directly quoting Jesus.

"Come to me, all you who are weary and burdened, and I will give you rest. Take my yoke upon you and learn from me, for I am gentle and humble in heart, and you will find rest for your souls. For my yoke is easy and my burden is light." Matthew 11:28-30

When Jesus says come to me, He isn't calling us to a location, He is calling us into relationship with Himself. He invites us to come to Him and experience His rest, rest for our souls. When Jesus left Heaven and came to earth to be Immanuel, God with us, He traveled most of the distance to bridge the gap between us. He simply asks us to take a step towards Him. Oh friends, this Christmas, let's accept His invitation. Come to Jesus, and find rest in Him.

**PRAY:**
*Father God, thank You for the holy rhythm You established, setting the example of work and rest. Help me to develop good habits of daily and weekly rest. Lord, I accept Your invitation to come to Jesus and find rest in You. In Jesus' name, amen.*

# Way 12- You: Find Rest

**MEDITATE OR MEMORIZE:**
"It is in vain that you rise up early and go late to rest, eating the bread of anxious toil; for he gives to his beloved sleep." Psalm 127:2 (ESV)

"There are six days when you may work, but the seventh day is a day of sabbath rest, a day of sacred assembly. You are not to do any work; wherever you live, it is a sabbath to the Lord." Leviticus 23:3

"Come to me, all you who are weary and burdened, and I will give you rest." Matthew 11:28

**CONSIDER:**
1. Have you ever confused rest with laziness? In what way?

2. What role does daily rest play in your life?

3. In what practical ways can you experience rest for your mind?

4. Explain what sabbath rest means and how you can live it out.

5. What would it look like for you to accept the invitation to come to Jesus and find rest in Him?

# CONCLUSION:

# 12 Ways for Every Day

It took me a while to catch on, but maybe you already realized it. Call me Captain Obvious, but I did not understand the full implication of this message until I sat down to fully process "Our First Best Christmas." Peace on earth and joy to the world are not just for Christmastime. The principles in this book are *12 Ways for Every Day*.

Our tendencies to follow the pattern of the world are not exclusive to the holidays. We live in a culture driven to plan, prepare, and purchase our way to a better life throughout the year. We need to let God make us new by transforming our minds seasonally, monthly, weekly, and daily. To have the right priorities for our whole lives, we must continue to keep Jesus first, put others' needs above our own, and care for ourselves in a balanced way.

Love God. Love Others. Love Yourself.

The world's pattern is to leave Christmas behind on December 26th. A renewed mind knows the truth of Christmas is relevant every day! The *12 Ways of Christmas* are a pattern for living our lives year-round. We can employ these practical steps to make every season more restful and less stressful. In fact, if you're a New Year's resolution kind

# 12 Ways of Christmas

of person, you can view this as a jump start. We've already practiced for the month of December, so look out, January! But be aware, most New Year's resolutions are ditched in the first month. That's because, despite all our previous failed attempts, each January first, we decide to improve everything in our lives all at once.

Jesus is absolutely in the business of miraculously, instantaneously changing lives. He also causes transformation to happen in small, sustainable, incremental improvements as we partner with Him and walk in step with His Spirit to cultivate a new life in Christ.

Let's take a quick look at how we can live out the *12 Ways* all the time.

### Jesus

Jesus wants to be the center—not just of our holiday festivities, but of our entire lives. Let's go beyond the birthday month and celebrate Him all year! To *Make Room* for Jesus means we don't just squeeze Him in, but we invite Him in and always make Jesus our priority. To *Seek Him* looks like actively pursuing relationship with God daily. To *Worship Him* includes continually turning our hearts to Him in reverence and adoration. To *Surrender to Him* is to make Jesus our Lord, to trust God with our lives, and to release control.

### Others

A transformed life enables us to live others-focused every day. To *Be Present* occurs when we choose what is better, live in the moment, and be fully engaged with the people God has given us. To *Spread the Word* is lived out by sharing the good news about Jesus with others whenever we have the opportunity. To *Give Intentionally* means to be purposeful as we give gifts and to give charitably throughout the year. To *Serve Selflessly* is love in action, honoring others' needs above our own in every season.

## You

We cannot love God with all our heart and soul and mind and strength unless we are healthy in those areas. We cannot love others well if we are depleted. New life in Christ frees us from the world's pattern of floundering between self-hatred and self-obsession. We don't have to choose between neglect and narcissism. There is another option, as we are transformed by the renewing of our minds, God invites us to care for ourselves in a balanced way.

To *Prepare Your Heart* means to partner with God as He performs the cultivating work that continues to help us look more like Jesus. We *Choose Joy* by making the daily, conscious decision to walk in step with the Spirit, choosing to cultivate the fruit He produces. To *Pursue Peace* is to earnestly desire, search for, and chase after spiritual wholeness. To *Find Rest* happens when we intentionally carve out space for renewal in your body, mind, and soul.

## Abundant Life

Jesus did not leave Heaven, take on human form, and come to earth just to give us a new holiday to celebrate. He came to give us new life in Him! Through relationship with Jesus, we are new creations. We are no longer bound to conform to the world's pattern, we are free to live transformed lives!

Jesus said, "The thief comes only to steal and kill and destroy; I have come that they may have life, and have it to the full." John 10:10

# 12 Ways of Christmas

There is a real enemy of our souls. The thief cannot snatch us from Jesus' hand, but he makes every effort to keep us living defeated lives. Jesus, in contrast, came to bring us full life (some translations say abundant life) in Him!

Jesus does not promise a problem-free life, but one of assurance that He will never leave us or forsake us. Even when our circumstances do not feel good, He will work all things together for our good and for His glory. While we will always have trouble in this world, we can take heart that He has overcome the world! The transformed, abundant life Jesus offers is not just a promise for the afterlife. Eternity begins here and now.

# About the Author

Cassia Elder is an author, speaker, and founder of *Sisters Forward*. She lives in Southern Indiana on a nearly-off-grid microfarm with her husband Chris, their son Asa, and a porch-sittin' hound dog named Moonshine. Their days are spent restoring a rustic log cabin on the creek and exploring nature.

Most mornings you'll find Cassia rocking in her Grandma Phyllis's hand-me-down glider on the back porch with a mug of coffee in her hand and a Bible in her lap. She is a nerd for God's Word who enjoys gardening and has been passionate about crafting with words since joining the Young Author's Club in the fourth grade.

Cassia is overjoyed to connect with an online audience where she has conversations about real life, engages with Scripture, and navigates the practical application of how those two things fit together. What fills her cup most is to have these authentic conversations with women in person—at events, conferences, retreats, any place women gather—to hug their necks, hear their stories, and share the truth of God's Word.

**Website:** cassiaelder.com

**Facebook:** https://www.facebook.com/eldercassia/
https://www.facebook.com/sistersforward

**Instagram:** https://www.instagram.com/cassiaelder/
https://www.instagram.com/sistersforward

# Also from Cassia

Do you want to make a difference, but wonder if your day-to-day life really matters?

The term "blessed" gets tossed around flippantly. Overuse and misuse have rendered it nearly meaningless. It has been dwindled down to infer being merely fortunate, lucky. #FeelingBlessed! So what does blessing really look like? *Make Me a Blessing* redeems the meaning of the word blessed, acknowledges how blessed we are, and reminds us of the reason why. **We are blessed to be a blessing.**

In *Make Me a Blessing* you will:
* Discover Right Now Purpose in your circle of influence.
* Practice gratitude, the catalyst to blessing.
* Overcome the #1 enemy of blessing—self-focus.
* Participate in the Blessing Cycle in practical ways.
* Pray. Encourage. Give. Serve. Share. Inspire.

**Dig deeper with this:
8-SESSION COMPANION
STUDY GUIDE**

Made in the USA
Middletown, DE
12 October 2022